The Live Corpse

Leo Tolstoy

Translator: Louise Maude,

Aylmer Maude

Contents

THE LIVE CORPSE

BY

Leo Tolstoy

Translator: Louise Maude, Aylmer Maude

THE LIVE CORPSE

A PLAY IN SIX ACTS

CHARACTERS

THEODORE VASÍLYEVICH PROTÁSOV (FÉDYA).

ELISABETH ANDRÉYEVNA PROTÁSOVA (LISA). His wife.

MÍSHA. Their son.

ANNA PÁVLOVNA. Lisa's mother.

SÁSHA. Lisa's younger, unmarried sister.

VICTOR MIHÁYLOVICH KARÉNIN.

ANNA DMÍTRIEVNA KARÉNINA.

PRINCE SERGIUS DMÍTRIEVICH ABRÉZKOV.

MÁSHA. A gipsy girl.

IVÁN MAKÁROVICH. An old gipsy man. }
                                                          } Másha's parents.

NASTÁSIA IVÁNOVNA. An old gipsy woman. }

OFFICER.

MUSICIAN.

FIRST GIPSY MAN.

SECOND GIPSY MAN.

GIPSY WOMAN.

GIPSY CHOIR.

DOCTOR.

MICHAEL ALEXÁNDROVICH AFRÉMOV.

STÁKHOV.   }
                                                  }
BUTKÉVICH.   } Fédya's boon companions.
                                                  }
KOROTKÓV.   }

IVÁN PETRÓVICH ALEXÁNDROV.

VOZNESÉNSKY. Karénin's secretary.

PETUSHKÓV. An artist.

ARTÉMYEV.

WAITER IN THE PRIVATE ROOM AT THE RESTAURANT.

WAITER IN A LOW-CLASS RESTAURANT.

MANAGER OF THE SAME.

POLICEMAN.

INVESTIGATING MAGISTRATE.

MÉLNIKOV.

CLERK.

USHER.

YOUNG LAWYER.

PETRÚSHIN. A lawyer.

LADY.

ANOTHER OFFICER.

ATTENDANT AT LAW COURTS.

THE PROTÁSOVS' NURSE.

THE PROTÁSOVS' MAID.

AFRÉMOV'S FOOTMAN.

KARÉNIN'S FOOTMAN.

THE LIVE CORPSE

ACT I

SCENE 1

Protásov's[1] flat in Moscow. The scene represents a small dining-room.

[1] Protásov is his family name, but the name by which he is usually addressed is Fédya, an abbreviation of his Christian name--Theodore. The ceremonious form of address would be Theodore Vasílyevich.

Anna Pávlovna, a stout grey-haired lady, tightly laced, is sitting alone at the tea-table on which is a samovár. Enter nurse, carrying a teapot.

NURSE. May I have a little hot water, ma'am?

ANNA PÁVLOVNA. Yes. How's Baby?

NURSE. He's restless.... There's nothing worse than for a lady to nurse her baby herself! She has her troubles, and the child must suffer. What can her milk be like, when she lies awake crying all night?

ANNA PÁVLOVNA. But she seems quieter now.

NURSE. Quiet, indeed! It makes one ill to see her. She's been writing something, and crying.

    Enter Sásha.

SÁSHA [to Nurse] Lisa is looking for you.

NURSE. I'm coming, I'm coming. [Exit].

ANNA PÁVLOVNA. Nurse says she keeps on crying.... Why can't she control herself?

SÁSHA. Well really, mother, you are amazing!... A woman has left her husband, her child's father, and you expect her to be calm!

ANNA PÁVLOVNA. Well, not calm ... But what's done is done! If I, her mother, not only allowed my daughter to leave her husband, but am even glad she has done it, that shows he deserved it. One ought to rejoice, not to grieve, at the chance of freeing oneself from such a bad man!

SÁSHA. Mother, why say such things? You know it's not true! He's not bad--but on the contrary, he's a wonderful man, in spite of his weaknesses.

ANNA PÁVLOVNA. Yes indeed, a "wonderful" man--as soon as he has money in
his pocket--his own or other people's....

SÁSHA. Mother! He has never taken other people's!

ANNA PÁVLOVNA. Yes he has--his wife's! Where's the difference?

SÁSHA. But he gave all his property to his wife!

ANNA PÁVLOVNA. Of course, when he knew that otherwise he was sure to squander it all!

SÁSHA. Squander or not, I only know that a wife must not separate from her husband, especially from such a one as Fédya.

ANNA PÁVLOVNA. Then, in your opinion she ought to wait till he has squandered everything, and brought his gipsy mistresses into the house?

SÁSHA. He has no mistresses!

ANNA PÁVLOVNA. That's the misfortune--he seems to have bewitched you all! But not me--no! He won't come over me! I see through him, and he knows it. Had I been in Lisa's place I should have left him a year ago.

SÁSHA. How lightly you say it!

ANNA PÁVLOVNA. Not lightly at all. It's not a light thing for me, as a mother, to see my daughter divorced. Believe me it's not! But yet it is better than ruining a young life.... No, I'm thankful to God that she has at last made up her mind, and that it is all over.

SÁSHA. Perhaps it's not all over!

ANNA PÁVLOVNA. Oh! If he only consents to a divorce....

SÁSHA. What good will that do?

ANNA PÁVLOVNA. This good; that she is young, and may again be happy.

SÁSHA. Oh mother! It's dreadful to hear you speak so! Lisa can't love another.

ANNA PÁVLOVNA. Why not, when she's free? Many a man a thousand times better than your Fédya might turn up who would be only too happy to marry Lisa.

SÁSHA. Mother, it's not right! I know you're thinking of Victor Karénin....

ANNA PÁVLOVNA. And why shouldn't I? He has loved her these ten years, and she loves him.

SÁSHA. Yes, but not as a husband! They have been friends from childhood.

ANNA PÁVLOVNA. We know those friendships! If only the obstacles were out of the way!

    Enter Maid.

ANNA PÁVLOVNA. What is it?

MAID. The mistress has sent the porter with a note for Mr. Karénin.

ANNA PÁVLOVNA. What mistress?

MAID. *Our* mistress--Mrs. Protásova.

ANNA PÁVLOVNA. Well?

MAID. Mr. Karénin has sent back word that he will come round at once.

ANNA PÁVLOVNA [surprised] We were just speaking of him! Only I can't think why ... [to Sásha] Do you know?

SÁSHA. Perhaps I do, and perhaps I don't!

ANNA PÁVLOVNA. You always have secrets!

SÁSHA. Lisa will tell you herself when she comes.

ANNA PÁVLOVNA [shakes her head. To Maid] The samovár must be made to boil again. Take it, Dounyásha.

　　　Maid takes samovár, and exit.

ANNA PÁVLOVNA [to Sásha who has risen and is going out] It turns out just as I told you! She sent for him at once....

SÁSHA. She may have sent for him for quite a different reason.

ANNA PÁVLOVNA. What for, then?

SÁSHA. Now, at this moment, Karénin is the same to her as old Nurse Trífonovna.

ANNA PÁVLOVNA. Well, you'll see.... Don't I know her? She has sent for him to comfort her.

SÁSHA. Oh mother, how little you know her, to be able to suppose ...!

ANNA PÁVLOVNA. Well, we'll see!... And I am very, very glad.

SÁSHA. We *shall* see! [Exit, humming a tune].

ANNA PÁVLOVNA [alone, shakes her head and mutters] It's all right, it's all right!

Enter Maid.

MAID. Mr. Karénin has come.

ANNA PÁVLOVNA. Well then, show him in, and tell your mistress.

Maid exit by inner door. Enter Karénin, who bows to Anna Pávlovna.

KARÉNIN. Your daughter wrote to me to come. I meant to come and see you to-night, anyhow. So I was very pleased ... Is Elisabeth Andréyevna[2] well?

[2] Elisabeth Andréyevna is the polite way of speaking of Mrs. Protásova, otherwise Lisa.

ANNA PÁVLOVNA. Yes, she is well, but Baby is a bit restless. She will be here directly. [In a melancholy voice] Ah yes! It is a sad time.... But you know all about it, don't you?

KARÉNIN. I do. I was here, you know, the day before yesterday, when his letter came. But is it possible that everything is irrevocably settled?

ANNA PÁVLOVNA. Why of course! Naturally! To go through it all again would be intolerable.

KARÉNIN. This is a case where the proverb applies: "Measure ten times before you cut once." ... It is very painful to cut into the quick.

ANNA PÁVLOVNA. Of course it is; but then their marriage has long had a rift in it, so that the tearing asunder was easier than one would have thought. He himself sees that, after what has occurred, it is impossible for him to return.

KARÉNIN. Why so?

ANNA PÁVLOVNA. How can you expect it, after all his horrid goings-on--after he swore it should not happen again, and that if it did he would renounce all rights as a husband and set her perfectly free?

KARÉNIN. Yes, but how can a woman be free when she is bound by marriage?

ANNA PÁVLOVNA. By divorce. He promised her a divorce, and we shall insist on it.

KARÉNIN. Yes, but Elisabeth Andréyevna loved him so....

ANNA PÁVLOVNA. Ah, but her love has suffered such trials that there can hardly be anything left of it! Drunkenness, deception, and infidelity ... Can one love such a husband?

KARÉNIN. Nothing is impossible to love.

ANNA PÁVLOVNA. You talk of love! But how can one love such a man--a broken reed, whom one can never depend on? Don't you know what it came to ...? [Looks round at the door, and continues hurriedly] All his affairs in a muddle, everything pawned, nothing to pay with! Then their uncle sends 2,000 roubles to pay the interest on their mortgaged estates, and he takes the money and disappears. His wife is left at home, with a sick baby, waiting for him--and at last gets a note asking her to send him his clothes and things!

KARÉNIN. Yes, yes; I know.

Enter Lisa and Sásha.

ANNA PÁVLOVNA. Well, here is Victor Miháylovich,[3] obedient to your summons.

[3] The polite way of naming Mr. Karénin.

KARÉNIN. Yes, but I am sorry I was delayed for a few minutes.

LISA. Thank you. I have a great favour to ask of you, and I have no one to turn to but you.

KARÉNIN. Anything in my power ...

LISA. You know all about ...?

KARÉNIN. I do.

ANNA PÁVLOVNA. Well then, I shall leave you [To Sásha] Come, we'll leave them alone. [Exit with Sásha].

LISA. Yes, he wrote to me saying that he considers everything at an end ... [struggling with her tears] ... and I was hurt!... and so ... In a word, I consented to break--I answered, accepting his renunciation.

KARÉNIN. And now you repent?

LISA. Yes. I feel that I was wrong, and that I cannot do it. Anything is better than to be separated from him. In short--I want you to give him this letter.... Please, Victor, give him the letter, and tell him ...

and bring him back!

KARÉNIN [surprised] Yes, but how?

LISA. Tell him I ask him to forget everything, and to return. I might simply send the letter, but I know him: his first impulse, as always, will be the right one--but then someone will influence him, and he'll change his mind and not do what he really wants to....

KARÉNIN. I will do what I can.

LISA. You're surprised at my asking *you*?

KARÉNIN. No.... Yet, to tell you the truth--yes, I am surprised.

LISA. But you are not angry?

KARÉNIN. As if I could be angry with you!

LISA. I asked you because I know you care for him.

KARÉNIN. Him, and you too! You know that. I am thinking not of myself, but of you. Thank you for trusting me! I will do what I can.

LISA. I know.... I will tell you everything. To-day I went to Afrémov's to find out where he was. I was told he had gone to the gipsies--which is what I feared most of all. I know he will get carried away if he is not stopped in time--and that's what has to be done.... So you'll go?

KARÉNIN. Of course, and at once.

LISA. Go!... Find him, and tell him all is forgotten and I am waiting for him.

KARÉNIN. But where am I to look for him?

LISA. He is with the gipsies. I went there myself.... I went as far as the porch, and wished to send in the letter, but changed my mind and decided to ask you. Here is the address.... Well, then, tell him to return: tell him nothing has happened ... all is forgotten. Do it for love of him, and for the sake of our friendship!

KARÉNIN. I will do all in my power! [Bows, and exit].

LISA. I can't, I can't! Anything rather than ... I can't!

    Enter Sásha.

SÁSHA. Well, have you sent?

    Lisa nods affirmatively.

SÁSHA. And he agreed?

LISA. Of course.

SÁSHA. But why just *him*? I don't understand.

LISA. But who else?

SÁSHA. Don't you know he is in love with you?

LISA. That's dead and gone. Whom would you have had me send?... Do you think he *will* come back?

SÁSHA. I am sure of it, because ...

Enter Anna Pávlovna. Sásha is silent.

ANNA PÁVLOVNA. And where is Victor Miháylovich?

LISA. He's gone.

ANNA PÁVLOVNA. Gone! How's that?

LISA. I asked him to do something for me.

ANNA PÁVLOVNA. "Do something?" Another secret!

LISA. It's not a secret. I simply asked him to give a letter into Fédya's own hands.

ANNA PÁVLOVNA. Fédya? What--to Theodore Vasílyevich?

LISA. Yes, to Fédya.

ANNA PÁVLOVNA. I thought all relations between you were over!

LISA. I can't part from him.

ANNA PÁVLOVNA. What? Are you going to begin all over again?

LISA. I wanted to, and tried ... but I can't! Anything you like--only I can't part from him!

ANNA PÁVLOVNA. Then do you want to have him back again?

LISA. Yes.

ANNA PÁVLOVNA. To let that skunk into the house again?

LISA. Mother, I beg you not to speak so of my husband!

ANNA PÁVLOVNA. He *was* your husband.

LISA. No, he is my husband still.

ANNA PÁVLOVNA. A spendthrift, a drunkard, a rake ... and you can't part from him?

LISA. Why do you torment me! You seem to want to do it.... It's hard enough for me without that.

ANNA PÁVLOVNA. I torment you! Well then, I'll go. I can't stand by and see it....

　　Lisa is silent.

ANNA PÁVLOVNA. I see! That's just what you want--I'm in your way.... I can't live so. I can't make you out at all! It's all so new-fangled--first you make up your mind to separate, then you suddenly send for a man who is in love with you ...

LISA. Nothing of the kind.

ANNA PÁVLOVNA. Karénin proposed to you ... and you send him to fetch your husband! Why? To arouse jealousy?

LISA. Mother, what you are saying is terrible! Leave me alone!

ANNA PÁVLOVNA. Very well! Turn your mother out of the house, and let in your rake of a husband!... Yes, I will not remain here! Good-bye, then--I leave you to your fate; you can do as you please! [Exit slamming door].

LISA [drops into a chair] That's the last straw!

SÁSHA. Never mind.... It will be all right; we'll soon pacify Mother.

ANNA PÁVLOVNA [passing through] Dounyásha! My trunk!

SÁSHA. Mother, listen!... [follows her out with a significant glance to Lisa].

Curtain.

SCENE 2

A room in the gipsies' house. The choir is singing "Kanavela." Fédya in his shirt-sleeves is lying prone on the sofa. Afrémov sits astride a chair in front of the leader of the choir. An officer sits at a table, on which are bottles of champagne and glasses. A musician is taking notes.

AFRÉMOV. Fédya, are you asleep?

FÉDYA [rising] Don't talk.... Now let's have "Not at Eve."

GIPSY LEADER. That won't do, Theodore Vasílyevich! Let Másha sing a solo now.

FÉDYA. All right! And then, "Not at Eve." [Lies down again].

OFFICER. Sing "Fateful Hour."

GIPSY. All agreed?

AFRÉMOV. Go on!

OFFICER [to musician] Have you taken it down?

MUSICIAN. Quite impossible! It's different every time.... And the scale is somehow different. Look here! [Beckons to a gipsy woman who is looking on] Is this right? [Hums].

GIPSY. That's it, that's splendid!

FÉDYA. He'll never get it; and if he does take it down and shoves it into an opera, he'll only spoil it!... Now, Másha, start off! Let's have "Fateful Hour"--take your guitar. [Rises, sits down opposite her, and gazes into her eyes].

Másha sings.

FÉDYA. That's good too! Másha, you're a brick!... Now then, "Not at Eve"!

AFRÉMOV. No, wait! First, my burial song....

OFFICER. Why *burial*?

AFRÉMOV. Because, when I'm dead ... you know, dead and laid in my coffin, the gipsies will come (you know I shall leave instructions with my wife) and they will begin to sing "I Walked a Mile" ... and then I'll jump out of my coffin!... Do you understand? [To the musician] You just write this down. [To the gipsies] Well, rattle along!

Gipsies sing.

AFRÉMOV. What do you think of that?... Now then, "My Brave Lads"!

Gipsies sing.

Afrémov gesticulates and dances. The gipsies smile and continue singing, clapping their hands. Afrémov sits down and the song ends.

GIPSIES. Bravo! Michael Andréyevich![4] He's a real gipsy!

 [4] The polite way of addressing Mr. Afrémov.

FÉDYA. Well, *now* "Not at Eve"!

Gipsies sing.

FÉDYA. That's it! It's wonderful ... And where does it all happen--all that this music expresses? Ah, it's fine!... And how is it man can reach such ecstasy, and cannot keep it?

MUSICIAN [taking notes] Yes, it's most original.

FÉDYA. Not original--but the real thing!

AFRÉMOV [to gipsies] Well, have a rest now. [Takes the guitar and sits down beside Kátya, one of the gipsies].

MUSICIAN. It's really simple, except the rhythm....

FÉDYA [waves his hand, goes to Másha, and sits down on sofa beside her]

Oh, Másha, Másha! How you do turn me inside-out!

MÁSHA. And how about what I asked you for?

FÉDYA. What? Money?... [Takes some out of his trouser-pocket] Here, take it!

Másha laughs, takes it, and hides it in her bosom.

FÉDYA [to the gipsies] Who can make it out? She opens heaven for me, and then asks for money to buy scents with! [To Másha] Why, you don't in the least understand what you're doing!

MÁSHA. Not understand indeed! I understand that when I am in love, I try to please my man, and sing all the better.

FÉDYA. Do you love me?

MÁSHA. Looks like it!

FÉDYA. Wonderful! [Kisses her].

Exeunt most of the gipsies. Some couples remain: Fédya with Másha, Afrémov with Kátya, and the officer with Gásha. The musician writes. A gipsy man strums a valse tune on the guitar.

FÉDYA. But I'm married, and your choir won't allow it....

MÁSHA. The choir is one thing, one's heart's another! I love those I love, and hate those I hate.

FÉDYA. Ah! This is good! Isn't it?

MÁSHA. Of course it's good--we've jolly visitors, and are all merry.

Enter gipsy man.

GIPSY [to Fédya] A gentleman is asking for you.

FÉDYA. What gentleman?

GIPSY. I don't know.... Well dressed, wears a sable overcoat--

FÉDYA. A swell? Well, ask him in. [Exit Gipsy].

AFRÉMOV. Who has come to see you here?

FÉDYA. The devil knows! Who can want me?

Enter Karénin. Looks round.

FÉDYA. Ah, Victor! I never expected *you*!... Take off your coat!...
What wind has blown you here? Come, sit down and listen to "Not at Eve."

KARÉNIN. Je voudrais vous parler sans témoins.[5]

[5] I wanted to speak to you alone.

FÉDYA. What about?

KARÉNIN. Je viens de chez vous. Votre femme m'a chargé de cette lettre
et puis ...[6]

[6] I have come from your home. Your wife has entrusted me with this
letter and besides ...

FÉDYA [takes letter, reads, frowns, then smiles affectionately] I say, Karénin, of course you know what is in this letter?

KARÉNIN. I know ... and I want to say ...

FÉDYA. Wait, wait a bit! Please don't imagine that I am drunk and my words irresponsible.... I mean, that I am irresponsible! I am drunk, but in this matter I see quite clearly.... Well, what were you commissioned to say?

KARÉNIN. I was commissioned to find you, and to tell you ... that ... she ... is waiting for you. She asks you to forget everything and come back.

FÉDYA [listens in silence, gazing into Karénin's eyes] Still, I don't understand why *you* ...

KARÉNIN. Elisabeth Andréyevna sent for me, and asked me ...

FÉDYA. So ...

KARÉNIN. But I ask you, not so much in your wife's name as from myself.... Come home!

FÉDYA. You are a better man than I. (What nonsense! It is easy enough to be better than I) ... I am a scoundrel, and you are a good--yes, a good man.... And that is the very reason why I won't alter my decision.... No! Not on that account either--but simply because I can't and won't.... How could I return?

KARÉNIN. Let us go to my rooms now, and I'll tell her that you will return to-morrow.

FÉDYA. And to-morrow, what?... I shall still be I, and she--she. [Goes to the table and drinks] It's best to have the tooth out at one go.... Didn't I say that if I broke my word she was to throw me over? Well, I have broken it, and that's the end of it.

KARÉNIN. For you, but not for her!

FÉDYA. It is extraordinary that **you** should take pains to prevent our marriage being broken up!

KARÉNIN [is about to speak, but Másha comes up] ...

FÉDYA [interrupting him] Just hear her sing "The Flax"!... Másha!

The gipsies re-enter.

MÁSHA [whispers] An ovation, eh?

FÉDYA [laughs] An ovation!... "Victor, my Lord! Son of Michael!" ...

Gipsies sing a song of greeting and laudation.

KARÉNIN [listens in confusion then asks] How much shall I give them?

FÉDYA. Well, give them twenty-five roubles.[7]

[7] About £2, 10s.

Karénin gives the money.

FÉDYA. Splendid! And now, "The Flax!"

Gipsies sing.

FÉDYA [looks round] Karénin's bunked!... Well, devil take him!

> Gipsy group breaks up.

FÉDYA [sits down by Másha] Do you know who that was?

MÁSHA. I heard his name.

FÉDYA. He's an excellent fellow! He came to take me home to my wife. She loves a fool like me, and see what I am doing here ...!

MÁSHA. Well, and it's wrong! You ought to go back to her.... You ought to pity her.

FÉDYA. You think I ought to? Well, I think I ought not.

MÁSHA. Of course, if you don't love her you need not. Only love counts.

FÉDYA. And how do you know that?

MÁSHA. Seems I do!

FÉDYA. Well, kiss me then!... Now, let's have "The Flax" once more, and then finish up.

> Gipsies sing.

FÉDYA. Ah, how good it is! If only one hadn't to wake up!... If one could die so!

> Curtain.

ACT II

SCENE 1

Two weeks have passed since Act I. Anna Pávlovna and Karénin are discovered sitting in Lisa's dining-room. Enter Sásha.

KARÉNIN. Well, what news?

SÁSHA. The doctor says there is no danger at present, as long as he does not catch cold.

ANNA PÁVLOVNA. Yes, but Lisa is quite worn out.

SÁSHA. He says it's false croup, and a very mild attack. [Points to a basket]. What's that?

ANNA PÁVLOVNA. Grapes. Victor brought them.

KARÉNIN. Won't you have some?

SÁSHA. Yes, she likes grapes. She has become terribly nervous.

KARÉNIN. Naturally--after not sleeping for two nights, and not eating.

SÁSHA. And how about you.

KARÉNIN. That's quite another matter.

    Enter doctor and Lisa.

DOCTOR [impressively] Yes, that's it. Change it every half-hour if he's awake, but if he's asleep don't disturb him. You need not paint the throat. The room must be kept at its present temperature ...

LISA. But if he again begins to choke?

DOCTOR. He probably won't, but if he should, use the spray. And give him the powders: one in the morning and the other at night. I will give you the prescription now.

ANNA PÁVLOVNA. Have a cup of tea, doctor?

DOCTOR. No thanks.... My patients are expecting me.

    Sits down to the table. Sásha brings him paper and ink.

LISA. So you're sure it is not croup?

DOCTOR [smiling] Perfectly certain!

KARÉNIN [to Lisa] And now have some tea, or, better still, go and lie down!... Just see what you look like....

LISA. Oh, now I am alive again. Thank you, you are a true friend! [Presses his hand. Sásha moves away angrily] I am so grateful to you, dear friend! At such times one recog ...

KARÉNIN. What have I done? There's really no cause at all to thank me.

LISA. And who stopped up all night? Who fetched the very best doctor?

KARÉNIN. I am already fully rewarded by the fact that Mísha is out of danger; and above all by your kindness.

LISA [presses his hand again and laughs, showing him some money in her hand] That's for the doctor; but I never know how to give it....

KARÉNIN. Neither do I.

ANNA PÁVLOVNA. Don't know what?

LISA. How to give money to a doctor.... He has saved more than my life, and I give him money! It seems so unpleasant.

ANNA PÁVLOVNA. Let me give it. I know how. It's quite simple.

DOCTOR [rises and hands the prescription to Lisa] These powders are to be well mixed in a tablespoonful of boiled water ... [goes on talking].

> Karénin sits at the table drinking tea; Sásha and Anna Pávlovna come forward.

SÁSHA. I can't bear the way they go on! It's just as if she were in love with him.

ANNA PÁVLOVNA. Well, can it be wondered at?

SÁSHA. It's disgusting!

> Doctor takes leave of everybody, and exit. Anna Pávlovna goes with him.

LISA [to Karénin] He's so sweet now! As soon as even he was a little better he at once began to smile and crow. I must go to him, but I don't like leaving you.

KARÉNIN. You had better have a cup of tea, and eat something.

LISA. I don't want anything now. I am so happy after all that anxiety!... [Sobs].

KARÉNIN. There! You see how worn out you are!

LISA. I'm so happy!... Would you like to have a look at him?

KARÉNIN. Of course.

LISA. Then come with me. [Exeunt].

ANNA PÁVLOVNA [returning to Sásha] What are you looking so glum about?... I gave him the money quite well, and he took it.

SÁSHA. It's disgusting! She has taken him with her to the nursery. It's just as if he were her fiancé or her husband....

ANNA PÁVLOVNA. Whatever does it matter to you? Why need you get excited
about it? Did you mean to marry him yourself?

SÁSHA. I? Marry that pikestaff? I'd rather marry I don't know whom, than him! Such a thing never entered my head.... I am only disgusted that, after Fédya, Lisa can be so attracted by a stranger.

ANNA PÁVLOVNA. Not a stranger, but an old playfellow!

SÁSHA. Don't I see by their smiles and looks that they are in love?

ANNA PÁVLOVNA. Well, what is there to be surprised at in that? He shares her anxiety about her baby, shows sympathy and helps her ... and she feels grateful. Besides, why should she not love and marry Victor?

SÁSHA. That would be disgusting--disgusting....

Enter Karénin and Lisa. Karénin silently takes leave. Sásha goes of angrily.

LISA [to Anna Pávlovna] What's the matter with her?

ANNA PÁVLOVNA. I really don't know.

Lisa sighs, and is silent.

Curtain.

SCENE 2

Afrémov's sitting-room. Glasses of wine on the table. Afrémov, Fédya, Stákhov (shaggy), Butkévich (close-shaven), and Korotkóv (a tuft-hunter).

KOROTKÓV. And I tell you that he'll be out of the running! La Belle Bois is the best horse in Europe.... Will you bet?

STÁKHOV. Don't, my dear fellow.... You know very well that nobody believes you, or will bet with you.

KOROTKÓV. I tell you your Cartouche won't be in it!

AFRÉMOV. Stop quarrelling! Let me settle it ... ask Fédya--he'll give you the right tip.

FÉDYA. Both horses are good. All depends on the jockey.

STÁKHOV. Gúsev is a rascal, and needs a firm hand on him.

KOROTKÓV [shouts] No!

FÉDYA. Wait a bit--I'll settle your differences.... Who won the Moscow Derby?

KOROTKÓV. He did--but what of that? It was only chance. If Crakus had not fallen ill.... [Enter footman].

AFRÉMOV. What is it?

FOOTMAN. A lady has come, and is asking for Mr. Protásov.

AFRÉMOV. What is she like? A real lady?

FOOTMAN. I don't know her name, but she's a real lady.

AFRÉMOV. Fédya! a lady to see you!

FÉDYA [startled] Who is it?

AFRÉMOV. He doesn't know.

FOOTMAN. Shall I ask her into the dining-room?

FÉDYA. No, wait.... I'll go myself and see.

Exeunt Fédya and footman.

KOROTKÓV. Who can it be? It must be Másha.

STÁKHOV. Which Másha?

KOROTKÓV. The gipsy. She's in love with him, like a cat.

STÁKHOV. What a darling she is ...! And how she sings!

AFRÉMOV. Charming! Tanyúsha and she! They sang with Peter yesterday.

STÁKHOV. What a lucky fellow that is!

AFRÉMOV. Why? Because the girls are all sweet on him? Not much luck in that!

KOROTKÓV. I can't bear gipsies--nothing refined about them.

BUTKÉVICH. No, you can't say that!

KOROTKÓV. I'd give the whole lot for one French woman!

AFRÉMOV. Yes, we know you--and your æsthetics!... I'll go and see who it is. [Exit].

STÁKHOV. If it's Másha, bring her in here! We'll make her sing.... No, the gipsies aren't what they used to be. Tanyúsha, now--by Gad!

BUTKÉVICH. And I believe they're just the same.

STÁKHOV. Just the same? When instead of their own pieces they sing empty drawing-room songs?

BUTKÉVICH. Some drawing-room songs are very good.

KOROTKÓV. Will you bet I don't get them to sing a drawing-room song so that you won't know it from one of their own?

STÁKHOV. Korotkóv always wants to bet!

    Enter Afrémov.

AFRÉMOV. I say, you fellows, it's not Másha--and there's no room he can ask her into but this. Let us clear out to the billiard room. [Exeunt].

    Enter Fédya and Sásha.

SÁSHA [confused] Fédya, forgive me if it's unpleasant--but for God's sake hear me!... [Her voice trembles].

    Fédya walks up and down the room. Sásha sits down, and follows him with her eyes.

SÁSHA. Fédya! Come home!

FÉDYA. Just listen to me, Sásha ... I quite understand you, Sásha dear, and in your place I should do the same--I should try to find some way to bring back the old state of affairs. But if you were me, if--strange as it sounds--you, dear sensitive girl, were in my place ... you would certainly have done as I did, and have gone away and ceased to spoil someone else's life.

SÁSHA. Spoil? How? As if Lisa could live without you!

FÉDYA. Oh, Sásha dear! Dear heart!... She can, she can! And she will yet be happy--far happier than with me.

SÁSHA. Never!

FÉDYA. It seems so to you [Takes her hand] ... But that's not the point. The chief thing is, that *I* can't!... You know, one folds a piece of thick paper this way and that a hundred times and still it holds together; but fold it once more, and it comes in half.... So it was with Lisa and me. It hurts me too much to look into her eyes--and she feels the same, believe me!

SÁSHA. No, no!

FÉDYA. You say "No," but you yourself know that it is "Yes"!

SÁSHA. I can only judge by myself. If I were in her place, and you answered as you are doing, it would be dreadful!

FÉDYA. Yes, for *you* ... [Pause; both are agitated].

SÁSHA [rises] Must things really remain so?

FÉDYA. I suppose ...

SÁSHA. Fédya come back!

FÉDYA. Thank you, Sásha dear! You will always remain a precious memory to me.... But good-bye, dear heart!... Let me kiss you. [Kisses her forehead].

SÁSHA [agitated] No, I don't say good-bye, and I don't believe, and won't believe ... Fédya!

FÉDYA. Well then, listen! But give me your word that what I tell you, you won't repeat to anybody--do you promise?

SÁSHA. Of course!

FÉDYA. Well then, listen, Sásha.... It's true that I am her husband and the father of her child, but I am--superfluous! Wait, wait--don't reply.... You think I'm jealous? Not at all! In the first place, I have no right; secondly, I have no cause. Victor Karénin is her old friend and mine too. He loves her, and she him.

SÁSHA. No!

FÉDYA. She does--as an honest, moral woman can, who does not allow herself to love anyone but her husband. But she loves, and will love him when this obstacle [points to himself] is removed; and I will remove it, and they shall be happy! [His voice trembles].

SÁSHA. Fédya, don't talk like that!

FÉDYA. Why, you know very well that it's true! And I shall be glad of their happiness, and it's the best I can do. I shall not return, but shall give them their freedom.... Tell them so.... Don't answer--and good-bye!

Kisses her on the forehead, and opens the door for her.

SÁSHA. Fédya--you are wonderful!

FÉDYA. Good-bye, good-bye!... [Exit Sásha].

FÉDYA. Yes, yes.... That's the thing ... that's the thing!... [Rings].

Enter footman.

FÉDYA. Call your master.... [Exit footman].... And it's true--it's true.

Enter Afrémov.

FÉDYA. Come along!

AFRÉMOV. Have you settled matters?

FÉDYA. Splendidly! [Sings]

"And she swore by ev'ry power ..."

Splendidly!... Where are they all?

AFRÉMOV. They're playing billiards.

FÉDYA. That's right--we will too [Sings]

"Rest here, just an hour ..."

Come along!

Curtain.

ACT III

SCENE 1

Prince Abrézkov, a sixty-year-old bachelor with moustaches, a retired army man, elegant, very dignified and melancholy-looking. Anna Dmítrievna Karénina (Victor's mother), a fifty-year-old "grande dame" who tries to appear younger, and intersperses her remarks with French expressions.

Anna Dmítrievna's sitting-room, furnished with expensive simplicity, and filled with souvenirs.

Anna Dmítrievna is writing. Footman enters.

FOOTMAN. Prince Abrézkov ...

ANNA DMÍTRIEVNA. Yes, certainly ... [Turns round and touches herself up before the looking-glass].

Enter Abrézkov.

PRINCE ABRÉZKOV. J'espère que je ne force pas la consigne....[8] [Kisses her hand].

[8] I hope I am not forcing myself on you.

ANNA DMÍTRIEVNA. You know that vous êtes toujours le bienvenu[9]--and to-day especially! You got my note?

[9] You are always welcome.

PRINCE ABRÉZKOV. I did, and this is my answer.

ANNA DMÍTRIEVNA. Ah, my friend! I begin quite to despair. Il est positivement ensorcelé![10] I never before knew him so insistent, so obstinate, so pitiless, and so indifferent to me. He has quite changed since that woman dismissed her husband!

[10] He is positively bewitched!

PRINCE ABRÉZKOV. What are the facts? How do matters actually stand?

ANNA DMÍTRIEVNA. He wants to marry her come what may.

PRINCE ABRÉZKOV. And how about the husband?

ANNA DMÍTRIEVNA. He agrees to a divorce.

PRINCE ABRÉZKOV. Dear me!

ANNA DMÍTRIEVNA. And he, Victor, lends himself to it, with all the abominations--lawyers, proofs of guilt--tout ça est dégoutant![11] And it doesn't seem to repel him. I don't understand him--he was always so sensitive, so reserved ...

[11] It is all disgusting!

PRINCE ABRÉZKOV. He is in love! Ah, when a man really loves ...

ANNA DMÍTRIEVNA. Yes, but how is it that in our day love could be
pure--could be a loving friendship, lasting through life? That kind of
love I understand and value.

PRINCE ABRÉZKOV. Nowadays the young generation no longer contents it-
self
with those ideal relations. La possession de l'âme ne leur suffit
plus.[12] It can't be helped!... What can one do with him?

   [12] For them, to possess the soul is no longer enough.

ANNA DMÍTRIEVNA. You must not say that of **him**--but it's as if he were
under a spell. It's just as if he were someone else.... You know, I
called on her. He begged me so. I went there, did not find her in, and
left my card. Elle m'a fait demander si je ne pourrais la
recevoir;[13] and to-day [looks at the clock] at two o'clock, that is
in a few minutes' time, she will be here. I promised Victor I would
receive her, but you understand how I am placed! I am not myself at all;
and so, from old habit, I sent for you. I need your help!

   [13] She inquired whether I would receive her.

PRINCE ABRÉZKOV. Thank you.

ANNA DMÍTRIEVNA. This visit of hers, you understand, will decide the
whole matter--Victor's fate! I must either refuse my consent--but how
can I?

PRINCE ABRÉZKOV. Don't you know her at all?

ANNA DMÍTRIEVNA. I have never seen her. But I'm afraid of her. A good woman could not consent to leave her husband, and he a good man, too! As a fellow-student of Victor's he used to visit us, you know, and was very nice. But whatever he may be, quels que soient les torts qu'il a eus vis-à-vis d'elle,[14] one must not leave one's husband. She ought to bear her cross. What I don't understand is how Victor, with the convictions he holds, can think of marrying a divorced woman! How often--quite lately--he has argued warmly with Spítsin in my presence, that divorce was incompatible with true Christianity; and now he himself is going in for it! Si elle a pu le charmer à un tel point[15] ... I am afraid of her! But I sent for you to know what *you* have to say to it all, and instead of that I have been doing all the talking myself! What do you think of it? Tell me your opinion. What ought I to do? You have spoken with Victor?

[14] However he may have wronged her.

[15] If she has been able to charm him to such a degree ...

PRINCE ABRÉZKOV. I have: and I think he loves her. He has grown used to loving her; and love has got a great hold on him. He is a man who takes things slowly but firmly. What has once entered his heart will never leave it again; and he will never love anyone but her; and he can never be happy without her, or with anyone else.

ANNA DMÍTRIEVNA. And how willingly Várya Kazántseva would have married
him! What a girl she is, and how she loves him!

PRINCE ABRÉZKOV [smiling]. C'est compter sans son hôte![16] That is quite out of the question now. I think it's best to submit, and help him to get married.

[16] That's reckoning without your host!

ANNA DMÍTRIEVNA. To a divorced woman--and have him meet his wife's husband?... I can't think how you can speak of it so calmly. Is she a woman a mother could wish to see as the wife of her only son--and such a son?

PRINCE ABRÉZKOV. But what is to be done, my dear friend? Of course it would be better if he married a girl whom you knew and liked; but since that's impossible ... Besides it's not as if he were going to marry a gipsy, or goodness knows who ...! Lisa Protásova is a very nice good woman. I know her, through my niece Nelly, and know her to be a modest, kind-hearted, affectionate and moral woman.

ANNA DMÍTRIEVNA. A moral woman--who makes up her mind to leave her husband!

PRINCE ABRÉZKOV. This is not like you! You're unkind and harsh! Her husband is the kind of man of whom one says that they are their own worst enemies; but he is an even greater enemy to his wife. He is a weak, fallen, drunken fellow. He has squandered all his property and hers too. She has a child.... How can you condemn her for leaving such a man? Nor has she left him: he left her.

ANNA DMÍTRIEVNA. Oh, what mud! What mud! And I have to soil my hands with it!

PRINCE ABRÉZKOV. And how about your religion?

ANNA DMÍTRIEVNA. Of course, of course! To forgive, "As we forgive them that trespass against us." *Mais, c'est plus fort que moi!*[17]

[17] But it's beyond me!

PRINCE ABRÉZKOV. How could she live with such a man? If she had not loved anyone else she would have had to leave him. She would have had to, for her child's sake. The husband himself--an intelligent kind-hearted man when he is in his senses--advises her to do it....

Enter Victor, who kisses his mother's hand and greets Prince Abrézkov.

VICTOR. Mother, I have come to say this: Elisabeth Andréyevna will be here in a minute, and I beg, I implore you--if you still refuse your consent to my marriage ...

ANNA DMÍTRIEVNA [interrupting him] Of course I still refuse my consent ...

VICTOR [continues his speech and frowns] In that case I beg, I implore you, not to speak to her of your refusal! Don't settle matters negatively ...

ANNA DMÍTRIEVNA. I don't expect we shall mention the subject. For my part, I certainly won't begin.

VICTOR. And she is even less likely to. I only want you to make her acquaintance.

ANNA DMÍTRIEVNA. The one thing I can't understand is how you reconcile your desire to marry Mrs. Protásova, who has a husband living, with your religious conviction that divorce is contrary to Christianity.

VICTOR. Mother, this is cruel of you! Are we really so immaculate that we must always be perfectly consistent when life is so complex? Mother, why are you so cruel to me?

ANNA DMÍTRIEVNA. I love you. I desire your happiness.

VICTOR [to Prince Abrézkov] Prince!

PRINCE ABRÉZKOV. Of course you desire his happiness. But it is not easy for you and me, with our grey hairs, to understand the young; and it is particularly difficult for a mother grown accustomed to her own idea of how her son is to be happy. Women are all like that.

ANNA DMÍTRIEVNA. Yes, yes indeed! You are all against me! You may do it, of course. Vous êtes majeur.[18] ... But you will kill me!

[18] You are of age.

VICTOR. You are not yourself. This is worse than cruelty!

PRINCE ABRÉZKOV [to Victor] Be quiet, Victor. Your mother's words are always worse than her deeds.

ANNA DMÍTRIEVNA. I shall tell her how I think and feel, but I will do it without offending her.

PRINCE ABRÉZKOV. Of that I am sure.

Enter footman.

PRINCE ABRÉZKOV. Here she is.

VICTOR. I'll go.

FOOTMAN. Elisabeth Andréyevna Protásova.

VICTOR. I am going. *Please*, Mother! [Exit.]

Prince Abrézkov also rises.

ANNA DMÍTRIEVNA. Ask her in. [To Prince Abrézkov] No, you must please stay here!

PRINCE ABRÉZKOV. I thought you'd find a tête-à-tête easier.

ANNA DMÍTRIEVNA. No, I'm afraid ... [Is restless] If I want to be left tête-à-tête *with her, I will nod to you.* Cela dépendra.[19] ... To be left alone with her may make it difficult for me. But I'll do like that if ... [Makes a sign].

 [19] It will depend.

PRINCE ABRÉZKOV. I shall understand. I feel sure you will like her. Only be just.

ANNA DMÍTRIEVNA. How you are all against me!

Enter Lisa, in visiting dress and hat.

ANNA DMÍTRIEVNA [rising] I was sorry not to find you in, and it is kind of you to call.

LISA. I never dreamed that you'd be so good as to call.... I am so grateful to you for wishing to see me.

ANNA DMÍTRIEVNA [pointing to Prince Abrézkov] You are acquainted?

PRINCE ABRÉZKOV. Yes, certainly. I have had the pleasure of being introduced. [They shake hands and sit down] My niece Nelly has often mentioned you to me.

LISA. Yes, she and I were great friends [glancing timidly at Anna Dmítrievna], and we are still friendly. [To Anna Dmítrievna] I never expected that you would wish to see me.

ANNA DMÍTRIEVNA. I knew your husband well. He was friendly with Victor,
and used to come to our house before he left for Tambóv. I think it was there you married?

LISA. Yes, it was there we married.

ANNA DMÍTRIEVNA. But after his return to Moscow he never visited us.

LISA. Yes, he hardly went out anywhere.

ANNA DMÍTRIEVNA. And he never introduced you to me.

Awkward silence.

PRINCE ABRÉZKOV. The last time I met you was at the theatricals at the Denísovs'. They went off very well; and you were acting.

LISA. No ... Yes ... Of course ... I did act. [Silence again]. Anna Dmítrievna, forgive me if what I am going to say displeases you, but I can't and don't know how to dissemble! I have come because Victor Miháylovich said ... because he--I mean, because you wished to see me.... But it is best to speak out [with a catch in her voice] ... It is very hard for me.... But you are kind.

PRINCE ABRÉZKOV. I'd better go.

ANNA DMÍTRIEVNA. Yes, do.

Prince Abrézkov takes leave of both women, and exit.

ANNA DMÍTRIEVNA. Listen, Lisa ... I am very sorry for you, and I like you. But I love Victor. He is the one being I love in the world. I know his soul as I know my own. It is a proud soul. He was proud as a boy of seven.... Not proud of his name or wealth, but proud of his character and innocence, which he has guarded. He is as pure as a maiden.

LISA. I know.

ANNA DMÍTRIEVNA. He has never loved any woman. You are the first. I do not say I am not jealous. I am jealous. But we mothers--your son is still a baby, and it is too soon for you--we are prepared for that. I was prepared to give him up to his wife and not to be jealous--but to a wife as pure as himself ...

LISA. I ... have I ...

ANNA DMÍTRIEVNA. Forgive me! I know it was not your fault, but you are unfortunate. And I know him. Now he is ready to bear--and will bear--anything, and he would never mention it, but he would suffer. His wounded pride would suffer, and he would not be happy.

LISA. I have thought of that.

ANNA DMÍTRIEVNA. Lisa, my dear, you are a wise and good woman. If you love him you must desire his happiness more than your own. And if that is so, you will not wish to bind him and give him cause to repent--though he would never *say* a word.

LISA. I know he wouldn't! I have thought about it, and have asked myself that question. I have thought of it, and have spoken of it to him. But what can I do, when he says he does not wish to live without me? I said to him: "Let us be friends, but do not spoil your life; do not bind your pure life to my unfortunate one!" But he does not wish for that.

ANNA DMÍTRIEVNA. No, not at present....

LISA. Persuade him to leave me, and I will agree. I love him for his own happiness and not for mine. Only help me! Do not hate me! Let us lovingly work together for his happiness!

ANNA DMÍTRIEVNA. Yes, yes! I have grown fond of you. [Kisses her. Lisa cries] And yet, and yet it is dreadful! If only he had loved you before you married ...

LISA. He says he did love me then, but did not wish to prevent a friend's happiness.

ANNA DMÍTRIEVNA. Ah, how hard it all is! Still, we will love one another, and God will help us to find what we want.

VICTOR [entering] Mother, dear! I have heard everything! I expected this: you are fond of her, and all will be well!

LISA. I am sorry you heard. I should not have said it if ...

ANNA DMÍTRIEVNA. Still, nothing is settled. All I can say is, that if it were not for all these unfortunate circumstances, I should have been glad. [Kisses her].

VICTOR. Only, please don't change!

Curtain.

SCENE 2

A plainly furnished room; bed, table, sofa. Fédya alone.

A knock at the door. A woman's voice outside. Why have you locked yourself in, Theodore Vasílyevich? Fédya! Open ...!

FÉDYA [gets up and unlocks door] That's right! Thank you for coming. It's dull, terribly dull!

MÁSHA. Why didn't you come to us? Been drinking again? Eh, eh! And after you'd promised!

FÉDYA. D'you know, I've no money!

MÁSHA. And why have I taken it into my head to care for you!

FÉDYA. Másha!

MÁSHA. Well, what about "Másha, Másha"? If you were really in love, you'd have got a divorce long ago. They themselves asked you to. You say you don't love her, but all the same you keep to her! I see you don't wish ...

FÉDYA. But you know why I don't wish!

MÁSHA. That's all rubbish. People say quite truly that you're an empty fellow.

FÉDYA. What can I say to you? That your words hurt me, you know without being told!

MÁSHA. Nothing hurts you!

FÉDYA. You know that the one joy I have in life is your love.

MÁSHA. *My* love--yes; but yours doesn't exist.

FÉDYA. All right. I'm not going to assure you. Besides, what's the good? You know!

MÁSHA. Fédya; why torment me?

FÉDYA. Which of us torments?

MÁSHA [cries] You are unkind!

FÉDYA [goes up and embraces her] Másha! What's it all about? Stop that. One must live, and not whine. It doesn't suit you at all, my lovely one!

MÁSHA. You do love me?

FÉDYA. Whom else could I love?

MÁSHA. Only me? Well then, read what you have been writing.

FÉDYA. It will bore you.

MÁSHA. It's you who wrote it, so it's sure to be good.

FÉDYA. Well then listen. [Reads] "One day, late in autumn, my friend and I agreed to meet on the Murýgin fields, where there was a close thicket with many young birds in it. The day was dull, warm, and quiet. The mist ..."

    Enter two old gipsies, Másha's parents, Iván Makárovich and Nastásia Ivánovna.

NASTÁSIA [stepping up to her daughter] Here you are then, you damned runaway sheep! [To Fédya] My respects to you, sir! [To Másha] Is that how you treat us, eh?

IVÁN [to Fédya] It's wrong, sir, what you're doing! You're ruining the wench! Oh, but it's wrong ... You're doing a dirty deed.

NASTÁSIA. Put on your shawl! March at once!... Running away like this! What can I say to the choir? Gallivanting with a beggar--what can you get out of him?

MÁSHA. I don't gallivant! I love this gentleman, that's all. I've not left the choir. I'll go on singing, and what ...

IVÁN. Say another word, and I'll pull the hair off your head!... Slut!... Who behaves like that? Not your father, nor your mother, nor your aunt!... It's bad, sir! We were fond of you--often and often we sang to you without pay. We pitied you, and what have you done?

NASTÁSIA. You've ruined our daughter for nothing ... our own, our only daughter, the light of our eyes, our priceless jewel--you've trodden her into the mire, that's what you've done! You've no conscience.

FÉDYA. Nastásia Ivánovna, you suspect me falsely. Your daughter is like a sister to me. I care for her honour. You must think no evil ... but I love her! What is one to do?

IVÁN. But you didn't love her when you had money! If you'd then subscribed ten thousand roubles or so to the choir, you might have had her honourably. But now you've squandered everything, and carry her off by stealth! It's a shame, sir, a shame!

MÁSHA. He has not carried me off! I came to him myself, and if you take me away now, I shall come back again. I love him, and there's an end of it! My love is stronger than all your locks ... I won't!

NASTÁSIA. Come, Másha dearest! Come, my own! Don't sulk. You've done wrong, and now come along.

IVÁN. Now then, you've talked enough! March! [Seizes her hand] Excuse us, sir! [Exit the three gipsies].

    Enter Prince Abrézkov.

PRINCE ABRÉZKOV. Excuse me. I have been an unwilling witness of an unpleasant scene....

FÉDYA. Whom have I the honour?... [Recognises the Prince] Ah, Prince Abrézkov! [They shake hands].

PRINCE ABRÉZKOV. An unwilling witness of an unpleasant scene. I should have been glad not to hear, but having overheard it, I consider it my duty to tell you so. I was directed here, and had to wait at the door for those people to come out--more particularly as their very loud voices rendered my knocking inaudible.

FÉDYA. Yes, yes--please take a seat. Thank you for telling me: it gives me the right to explain that scene to you. I don't mind what you may think of me, but I should like to tell you that the reproaches you heard addressed to that girl, that gipsy singer, were unjust. That girl is as morally pure as a dove; and my relations with her are those of a friend.

There may be a tinge of romance in them, but it does not destroy the purity--the honour--of the girl. That is what I wished to tell you; but what is it you want of me? In what way can I be of service?

PRINCE ABRÉZKOV. In the first place, I ...

FÉDYA. Forgive me, Prince. My present social standing is such, that my former slight acquaintance with you does not entitle me to a visit from you, unless you have some business with me. What is it?

PRINCE ABRÉZKOV. I won't deny it. You have guessed right. I have business with you; but I beg you to believe that the alteration in your position in no wise affects my attitude towards you.

FÉDYA. I am sure of it.

PRINCE ABRÉZKOV. My business is this. The son of my old friend, Anna Dmítrievna Karénina, and she herself, have asked me to ascertain directly from you what are your relations ... May I speak out?... your relations with your wife, Elisabeth Andréyevna Protásova.

FÉDYA. My relations with my wife, or rather with her who *was* my wife, are entirely at an end.

PRINCE ABRÉZKOV. So I understood, and that is why I accepted this difficult mission.

FÉDYA. At an end, and, I hasten to add, not by her fault, but by mine--by my innumerable faults. She is, as she always was, quite irreproachable.

PRINCE ABRÉZKOV. Well then, Victor Karénin, or rather his mother, asked me to find out what your intentions are.

FÉDYA [growing excited] What intentions? I have none. I set her quite free! Moreover, I will never disturb her peace. I know she loves Victor Karénin. Well, let her! I consider him a very dull, but very good and honourable man, and I think that she will, as the phrase goes, be happy with him; and--que le bon Dieu les bénisse![20] That's all ...

[20] May God bless them!

PRINCE ABRÉZKOV. Yes, but we ...

FÉDYA [interrupting] And don't suppose that I feel the least bit jealous. If I said that Victor is dull, I withdraw the remark. He is an excellent, honourable, moral man: almost the direct opposite of myself. And he has loved her from childhood. Perhaps she too may have loved him when she married me--that happens sometimes! The very best love is unconscious love. I believe she always did love him; but as an honest woman she did not confess it even to herself. But ... a shadow of some kind always lay across our family life--but why am I confessing to you?

PRINCE ABRÉZKOV. Please do! Believe me, my chief reason for coming to you was my desire to understand the situation fully.... I understand you. I understand that the shadow, as you so well express it, may have been ...

FÉDYA. Yes, it was; and that perhaps is why I could not find satisfaction in the family life she provided for me, but was always seeking something, and being carried away. However, that sounds like excusing myself. I don't want to, and can't, excuse myself. I was (I say with assurance, *was*) a bad husband. I say *was*, because in my consciousness I am not, and have long not been, her husband. I consider her perfectly free. So there you have my answer to your question.

PRINCE ABRÉZKOV. Yes, but you know Victor's family, and himself too. His relation to Elisabeth Andréyevna is, and has been all through, most respectful and distant. He assisted her when she was in trouble ...

FÉDYA. Yes, I by my dissipation helped to draw them together. What's to be done? It had to be so!

PRINCE ABRÉZKOV. You know the strictly Orthodox convictions of that family. Having myself a broader outlook on things, I do not share them; but I respect and understand them. I understand that for him, and especially for his mother, union with a woman without a Church marriage is unthinkable.

FÉDYA. Yes, I know his stu ... his strictness, his conservatism in these matters. But what do they want? A divorce? I told them long ago that I am quite willing; but the business of taking the blame on myself, and all the lies connected with it, are very trying....[21]

[21] Under the Russian law divorce was only obtainable if ocular evidence of adultery was forthcoming, and a great deal of perjury was usually involved in such cases.

PRINCE ABRÉZKOV. I quite understand you, and sympathise. But how can it be avoided? I think it might be arranged that way--but you are right. It is dreadful, and I quite understand you.

FÉDYA [pressing the Prince's hand] Thank you, dear Prince! I always knew you were a kind and honourable man. Tell me what to do. How am I to act? Put yourself in my place. I am not trying to improve. I am a good-for-nothing; but there are things I cannot do quietly. I cannot quietly tell lies.

PRINCE ABRÉZKOV. I don't understand you! You, a capable, intelligent man, so sensitive to what is good--how can you let yourself be so carried away--so forget what you expect of yourself? How have you ruined your life and come to this?

FÉDYA [forcing back tears of emotion] I have led this disorderly life for ten years, and this is the first time a man like you has pitied me! I have been pitied by my boon-companions, by rakes and by women; but a reasonable, good man like you ... Thank you! How did I come to my ruin? First, through drink. It is not that drink tastes nice; but do what I will, I always feel I am not doing the right thing, and I feel ashamed. I talk to you now, and feel ashamed. As for being a Maréchal de la noblesse, or a Bank Director--I should feel ashamed, so ashamed! It is only when I drink that I do not feel this shame. And music: not operas or Beethoven, but gipsies!... That is life! Energy flows into one's veins! And then those dear black eyes, and those smiles! And the more delicious it is, the more ashamed one feels afterwards.

PRINCE ABRÉZKOV. How about work?

FÉDYA. I have tried it, but it's no good. I am always dissatisfied with it--but what's the use of talking about myself! I thank you.

PRINCE ABRÉZKOV. Then what am I to say?

FÉDYA. Tell them I will do what they wish. They want to get married, and that there should be no obstacle to their marriage?

PRINCE ABRÉZKOV. Of course.

FÉDYA. I'll do it! Tell them I will certainly do it.

PRINCE ABRÉZKOV. But when?

FÉDYA. Wait a bit. Well, say in a fortnight. Will that do?

PRINCE ABRÉZKOV. Then I may tell them so?

FÉDYA. You may. Good-bye, Prince! Thank you once again!

[Exit Prince].

FÉDYA [sits for a long time and smiles silently] That's the way, that's the way! It must be so, must be, must be! Splendid!

Curtain.

ACT IV

SCENE 1

A private room in a restaurant. A waiter shows in Fédya and Iván Petróvich Alexándrov.

WAITER. Here, please. No one will disturb you here. I'll bring some paper directly.

IVÁN PETRÓVICH. Protásov, I'll come in too.

FÉDYA [seriously] If you like, but I'm busy and ... All right, come in.

IVÁN PETRÓVICH. You wish to reply to their demands? I'll tell you what to say. I should not do it that way--always speak straight out, and act with decision.

FÉDYA [to waiter] A bottle of champagne!

    Exit waiter.

FÉDYA [taking out a revolver and putting it on the table] Wait a bit!

IVÁN PETRÓVICH. What's that? Do you want to shoot yourself? You can if you like. I understand you! They wish to humiliate you, and you will show them the sort of man you are! You will kill yourself with a revolver, and them with magnanimity. I understand you. I understand everything, because I am a genius.

FÉDYA. Of course--of course. Only ... [Enter waiter with paper and ink].

FÉDYA [covers the revolver with a napkin] Uncork it--let's have a drink. [They drink. Fédya writes] Wait a bit!

IVÁN PETRÓVICH. Here's to your ... great journey! You know I'm above all this. I'm not going to restrain you! Life and death are alike to Genius. I die in life, and live in death. You will kill yourself that two people should pity you; and I--I shall kill myself that the whole world may understand what it has lost. I won't hesitate, or think about it! I seize it [snatches revolver]--now! And all is over. But it is too soon yet. [Lays down revolver] Nor shall I write anything; they must understand it themselves.... Oh, you ...

FÉDYA [writing] Wait a bit.

IVÁN PETRÓVICH. Pitiful people! They fuss, they bustle, and don't understand--don't understand anything at all.... I'm not talking to you, I am only expressing my thoughts. And, after all, what does humanity need? Very little--only to value its geniuses. But they always are executed, persecuted, tortured.... No! I'm not going to be your toy! I will drag you out into the open! No-o-o! Hypocrites!

FÉDYA [having finished writing, drinks and reads over his letter] Go away, please!

IVÁN PETRÓVICH. Go away? Well, good-bye then! I am not going to restrain you. I shall do the same. But not yet. I only want to tell you ...

FÉDYA. All right! You'll tell me afterwards. And now, dear chap, just one thing: give this to the manager [gives him money] and ask if a parcel and a letter have come for me.... Please do!

IVÁN PETRÓVICH. All right--then you'll wait for me? I have still something important to tell you--something that you will not hear in this world nor in the next, at any rate not till I come there.... Am I to let him have **all** of this?

FÉDYA. As much as is necessary. [Exit Iván Petróvich.]

Fédya sighs with relief; locks the door behind Iván Petróvich; takes up the revolver, cocks it, puts it to his temple; shudders, and carefully lowers it again. Groans.

FÉDYA. No; I can't! I can't! I can't! [Knock at the door] Who's there?

[Másha's voice from outside] It's me!

FÉDYA. Who's "me"? Oh, Másha ... [opens door].

MÁSHA. I've been to your place, to Popóv's, to Afrémov's, and guessed that you must be here. [Sees revolver] That's a nice thing! There's a fool! A regular fool! Is it possible you really meant to?

FÉDYA. No, I couldn't.

MÁSHA. Do I count for nothing at all? You heathen! You had no pity for me? Oh, Theodore Vasílyevich, it's a sin, a sin! In return for my love ...

FÉDYA. I wished to release them. I promised to, and I can't lie.

MÁSHA. And what about me?

FÉDYA. What about you? It would have set you free too. Is it better for you to be tormented by me?

MÁSHA. Seems it's better. I can't live without you.

FÉDYA. What sort of life could you have with me? You'd have cried a bit, and then gone on living your own life.

MÁSHA. I shouldn't have cried at all! Go to the devil, if you don't pity me! [Cries].

FÉDYA. Másha, dearest! I meant to do it for the best.

MÁSHA. Best for yourself!

FÉDYA [smiles] How's that, when I meant to kill myself?

MÁSHA. Of course, best for yourself! But what is it you want? Tell me.

FÉDYA. What I want? I want a great deal.

MÁSHA. Well, what? What?

FÉDYA. First of all, to keep my promise. That is the first thing, and quite sufficient. To lie, and do all the dirty work necessary to get a divorce ... I can't!

MÁSHA. Granted that it's horrid--I myself ...

FÉDYA. Next, they must really be free--my wife and he. After all, they are good people; and why should they suffer? That's the second thing.

MÁSHA. Well, there isn't much good in her, if she's thrown you over.

FÉDYA. She didn't--I threw her over.

MÁSHA. All right, all right! It's always you. She is an angel! What else!

FÉDYA. This--that you are a good, dear girlie--and that I love you, and if I live I shall ruin you.

MÁSHA. That's not your business. I know quite well what will ruin me.

FÉDYA [sighs] But above all, above all ... What use is my life? Don't I know that I am a lost good-for-nothing? I am a burden to myself and to everybody--as your father said. I'm worthless....

MÁSHA. What rubbish! I shall stick to you. I've stuck to you already, and there's an end of it! As to your leading a bad life, drinking and going on the spree--well, you're a living soul! Give it up, and have done with it!

FÉDYA. That's easily said.

MÁSHA. Well, then, do it.

FÉDYA. Yes, when I look at you I feel as if I could really do anything.

MÁSHA. And so you shall! Yes, you'll do it! [Sees the letter] What's that? You've written to them? What have you written?

FÉDYA. What have I written?... [Takes the letter and is about to tear it up] It's no longer wanted now.

MÁSHA [snatches the letter] You've said you would kill yourself? Yes? You did not mention the revolver--only said that you'd kill yourself?

FÉDYA. Yes, that I should be no more.

MÁSHA. Give it me--give it, give it!... Have you read **What to Do**?

FÉDYA. I think I have.

MÁSHA. It's a tiresome novel, but there's one very, very good thing in it. That what's his name?--Rakhmánov--goes and pretends he has drowned himself. And you--can you swim?

FÉDYA. No.

MÁSHA. That's all right. Let me have your clothes--everything, and your pocket-book too.

FÉDYA. How can I?

MÁSHA. Wait a bit, wait, wait! Let's go home; then you'll change your clothes.

FÉDYA. But it will be a fraud.

MÁSHA. All right! You go to bathe, your clothes remain on the bank, in the pocket is your pocket-book and this letter.

FÉDYA. Yes, and then?

MÁSHA. And then? Why, then we'll go off together and live gloriously.

Enter Iván Petróvich.

IVÁN PETRÓVICH. There now! And the revolver? I'll take it.

MÁSHA. Take it; take it! We're off.

Curtain.

SCENE 2

The Protásovs' drawing-room.

KARÉNIN. He promised so definitely, that I am sure he will keep his word.

LISA. I am ashamed to say it, but I must confess that what I heard about that gipsy girl makes me feel quite free. Don't think it is jealousy; it isn't, but you know--it sets me free. I hardly know how to tell you....

KARÉNIN. You don't know how to tell me ... Why?

LISA [smiling] Never mind! Only let me explain what I feel. The chief thing that tormented me was, that I felt I loved two men; and that meant that I was an immoral woman.

KARÉNIN. *You* immoral?

LISA. But since I knew that he had got someone else, and that he therefore did not need me, I felt free, and felt that I might truthfully say that I love you. Now things are clear within me, and only my position torments me. This divorce! It is such torture--and then this waiting!

KARÉNIN. It will soon, very soon, be settled. Besides his promise, I sent my secretary to him with the petition ready for signature, and told him not to leave till it is signed. If I did not know him so well, I should think he was purposely behaving as he does.

LISA. He? No, it is the result both of his weakness and his honesty. He doesn't want to say what is not true. Only you were wrong to send him money.

KARÉNIN. I had to. The want of it might be the cause of the delay.

LISA. No, there is something bad about money.

KARÉNIN. Well, anyhow, *he* need not have been so punctilious ...

LISA. How selfish we are becoming!

KARÉNIN. Yes, I confess it. It's your own fault. After all that waiting, that hopelessness, I am now so happy! And happiness makes one selfish. It's your fault!

LISA. Do you think it's you only? I too--I feel full of happiness, bathed in bliss! I have everything--Mísha has recovered, your mother likes me, and you--and above all, I, I love!

KARÉNIN. Yes? And no repenting? No turning back?

LISA. Since that day everything has changed in me.

KARÉNIN. And will not change again?

LISA. Never! I only wish you to have done with it all as completely as I have.

    Enter nurse, with baby. Lisa takes the baby on her lap.

KARÉNIN. What wretched people we are!

LISA [kissing baby] Why?

KARÉNIN. When you married, and I heard of it on my return from abroad, and was wretched because I felt that I had lost you, it was a relief to me to find that you still remembered me. I was content even with that. Then when our friendship was established and I felt your kindness to me, and even a little gleam of something in our friendship that was more than friendship, I was almost happy. I was only tormented by a fear that I was not being honest towards Fédya. But no! I was always so firmly conscious that any other relation than one of purest friendship with my friend's wife was impossible--besides which, I knew you--that I was not really troubled about that. Afterwards, when Fédya began to cause you anxiety, and I felt that I was of some use to you, and that my friendship was beginning to alarm you--I was quite happy, and a sort of vague hope awoke in me. Still later, when he became altogether impossible and you decided to leave him, and I spoke to you plainly for the first time, and you did not say "No," but went away in tears--then I was perfectly happy; and had I then been asked what more I wanted, I should have answered "Nothing"! But later on, when there came the possibility of uniting our lives: when my mother grew fond of you and the possibility began to be realised; when you told me that you loved and had loved me, and then (as you did just now) that he no longer existed for you and that you love only me--what more, one would think, could I wish for? But no! Now the past torments me! I wish that past had not existed, and that there were nothing to remind me of it.

LISA [reproachfully] Victor!

KARÉNIN. Lisa, forgive me! If I tell you this, it is only because I don't want a single thought of mine about you to be hidden from you. I have purposely told you, to show how bad I am, and how well I know that I must struggle with and conquer myself.... And now I've done it! I love him.

LISA. That's as it should be. I did all I could, but it was not I that did what you desired: it happened in my heart, from which everything but you has vanished.

KARÉNIN. Everything?

LISA. Everything, everything--or I would not say so.

    Enter footman.

FOOTMAN. Mr. Voznesénsky.

KARÉNIN. He's come with Fédya's answer.

LISA [to Karénin] Ask him in here.

KARÉNIN [rising and going to the door] Well, here is the answer!

LISA [gives baby to nurse; exit nurse] Is it possible, Victor, that everything will now be decided? [Kisses Karénin].

    Enter Voznesénsky.

KARÉNIN. Well?

VOZNESÉNSKY. He has gone.

KARÉNIN. Gone! And without signing the petition?

VOZNESÉNSKY. The petition is not signed, but a letter was left for you and Elisabeth Andréyevna [Takes letter out of his pocket and gives it to Karénin] I went to his lodgings, and was told he was at the restaurant. I went there, and Mr. Protásov told me to return in an hour and I should then have his answer. I went back, and then ...

KARÉNIN. Is it possible that this means another delay? More excuses! No, that would be downright wicked. How he has fallen!

LISA. But do read the letter! [Karénin opens letter].

VOZNESÉNSKY. You do not require me any longer?

KARÉNIN. Well, no. Good-bye! Thank you ... [Pauses in astonishment as he reads].

    Exit Voznesénsky.

LISA. What--what is it?

KARÉNIN. This is awful!

LISA [takes hold of letter] Read!

KARÉNIN [reads] "Lisa and Victor, I address myself to you both. I won't lie and call you 'dear' or anything else. I cannot master the feeling of bitterness and reproach (I reproach myself, but all the same it is painful) when I think of you and of your love and happiness. I know everything. I know that though I was the husband, I have--by a series of accidents--been in your way. *C'est moi qui suis l'intrus.*[22] But all the same, I cannot restrain a feeling of bitterness and coldness towards you. I love you both in theory, especially Lisa, Lisette! But actually I am more than cold towards you. I know I am wrong, but cannot change."

[22] It is I who am the intruder.

LISA. How can he ...

KARÉNIN [continues reading] "But to business! This very feeling of discord within me forces me to fulfil your desire not in the way you wish. Lying, acting so disgusting a comedy, bribing the Consistorium, and all those horrors, are intolerably repulsive to me. Vile as I may be, I am vile in a different way, and cannot take part in those abominations--simply cannot! The solution at which I have arrived is the simplest: to be happy, you must marry. I am in the way; consequently I must destroy myself...."

LISA [seizes Victor's hand] Victor!

KARÉNIN [reads] "... must destroy myself. And I will do it. When you get this letter, I shall be no more.

"*P.S.* What a pity you sent me money to pay for the divorce proceedings! It is unpleasant, and unlike you! But it can't be helped. I have so often made mistakes, why shouldn't you make one? I return the money. My way of escape is shorter, cheaper, and surer. All I ask is, don't be angry with me, and think kindly of me. And, one thing more--there is a clockmaker, Evgényev, here. Can't you help him, and set him on his feet? He's a good man, though weak.--Good-bye,

"FÉDYA."

LISA. He has taken his life! Yes ...

KARÉNIN [rings, and runs out to the hall] Call Mr. Voznesénsky back!

LISA. I knew it! I knew it! Fédya, dear Fédya!

KARÉNIN. Lisa!

LISA. It's not true, not true that I didn't love him and don't love him!
I love only him! I love him! And I've killed him. Leave me!

Enter Voznesénsky.

KARÉNIN. Where is Mr. Protásov? What did they tell you?

VOZNESÉNSKY. They told me he went out this morning, left this letter,
and had not returned.

KARÉNIN. We shall have to find out about it, Lisa. I must leave you.

LISA. Forgive me, but I too can't lie! Go now--go, and find out ...

Curtain.

ACT V

SCENE 1

A dirty room in a low-class restaurant. A table, at which people sit drinking tea and vódka. In the foreground a small table, at which sits Fédya, tattered, and much come down in the world. With him is Petushkóv, a gentle, mild man with long hair, of clerical appearance. Both are slightly drunk.

PETUSHKÓV. I understand, I understand. That is true love! Yes? Go on.

FÉDYA. Well, you know, if a woman of our class showed such feeling and sacrificed everything for the man she loved.... But she was a gipsy, brought up to money-hunting, and yet she had this self-sacrificing love! Gave everything, and wanted nothing herself! The contrast was so wonderful!

PETUSHKÓV. Yes, in art we call it "value." You can only get quite bright red by putting green round it. But that's not to the point. I understand, quite understand.

FÉDYA. Yes, and I believe the one good action of my life is that I never took advantage of her love. And do you know why?

PETUSHKÓV. Pity.

FÉDYA. Oh no! I never felt pity for her. What I felt for her was always rapturous admiration--and when she sang! Ah, how she sang--and perhaps still sings! I always regarded her as far above me. I did not ruin her, simply because I loved her; loved her truly. And now she's a good, happy memory! [Drinks].

PETUSHKÓV. Yes, I understand, I understand. It's ideal.

FÉDYA. I'll tell you something. I have had my passions, and once I was in love with a lady--very handsome--and I loved her nastily, like a dog. She gave me a *rendezvous*. And I did not go, because I thought it was treating the husband shabbily. And it is strange that, even now, when I remember it I want to feel pleased and to approve of myself for having acted honourably, but I always repent as if I had committed a sin! But in the case of Másha, on the contrary, I am always pleased--pleased that I did not pollute that feeling of mine.... I may fall lower still, sell all I have on me, be covered with lice and sores--but this jewel ... no, not jewel, but ray of sunshine, is still with me and in me.

PETUSHKÓV. I understand, I understand! And where is she now?

FÉDYA. I don't know! And I'd rather not know. All *that* belonged to a different life; and I don't want to mix it up with this....

> A woman is heard screaming at a table behind. The manager and a policeman come in and take her out. Fédya and Petushkóv listen, and look on in silence. When all is quiet again,

PETUSHKÓV. Yes, your life is astonishing.

FÉDYA. No, it's most simple! You know, in the society in which I was
born there are only three careers open to a man--only three. The first
is to enter the civil or military service, to earn money and increase
the abominations amid which we live. That was repulsive to me. Perhaps I
had not the capacity for it; but above all it repelled me. Then the
second is to destroy those abominations. To do that you must be a hero;
and I am not a hero. And the third is to forget it all by going on the
spree, drinking and singing. That is what I did. And this is what my
singing has brought me to! [Drinks].

PETUSHKÓV. And what about family life? I should be happy if I had a
wife. My wife ruined me.

FÉDYA. Family life? Yes, my wife was an ideal woman. She is still
living. But how shall I tell you? There was no yeast in it--you know,
the yeast that makes the beer froth! Well, there was nothing of that in
our life: it was flat, and I wanted something to help me to forget--and
one can't forget when there's no sparkle in life. Then I began to do all
sorts of nasty things. And you know, we love people for the good we do
them, and dislike them for the harm we do them; and I did her much harm.
She seemed to love me ...

PETUSHKÓV. Why do you say "seemed"?

FÉDYA. I say it because there was never anything about her that made her
creep into my soul as Másha did. But that's not what I meant to say.
When she was pregnant, or nursing her baby, I used to vanish, and come
home drunk; and of course, just because of that, I loved her less and
less. Yes, yes! [in ecstasy] I have it! The reason I love Másha is that
I did her good and not harm. That's why I love her. The other one I
tormented, and therefore I don't like her.... No, after all, I simply
don't like her! Was I jealous? Yes, but that too is past....

Enter Artémyev, with a cockade on his cap, dyed moustaches, and old renovated clothes.

ARTÉMYEV. Wish you a good appetite! [Bows to Fédya] I see you've made acquaintance with our painter, our artist.

FÉDYA [coldly] Yes, we are acquainted.

ARTÉMYEV [to Petushkóv] And have you finished the portrait?

PETUSHKÓV. No, I lost the order.

ARTÉMYEV [Sits down] I'm not in your way?

Fédya and Petushkóv do not answer.

PETUSHKÓV. Theodore Vasílyevich was telling me about his life.

ARTÉMYEV. Secrets? Then I won't disturb you--go on? I'm sure I don't want you. Swine! [Goes to next table and calls for beer. He listens all the time to Fédya's conversation with Petushkóv, and leans towards them without their noticing it.]

FÉDYA. I don't like that gentleman.

PETUSHKÓV. He was offended.

FÉDYA. Well, let him be! I can't stand him. He is such a fellow, my words won't come when he is there. Now with you I feel at ease, and comfortable. Well, what was I saying?

PETUSHKÓV. You were speaking about your jealousy. And how was it you parted from your wife?

FÉDYA. Ah! [Pauses and considers] It's a curious story. My wife is married ...

PETUSHKÓV. How's that? Are you divorced?

FÉDYA [smiles] No, I left her a widow.

PETUSHKÓV. What do you mean?

FÉDYA. I mean that she's a widow! I don't exist.

PETUSHKÓV. Don't exist?

FÉDYA. No, I'm a corpse! Yes ... [Artémyev leans over, listening] Well, you see--I *can* tell *you* about it; and besides, it happened long ago; and you don't know my real name. It was this way. When I had tired out my wife and had squandered everything I could lay my hands on, and had become unbearable, a protector turned up for her. Don't imagine that there was anything dirty or bad about it--no, he was my friend and a very good fellow--only in everything my exact opposite! And as there is far more evil than good in me, it follows that he was a good--a very good man: honourable, firm, self-restrained and, in a word, virtuous. He had known my wife from her childhood, and loved her. When she married me he resigned himself to his fate. But later, when I became horrid and tormented her, he began to come oftener to our house. I myself wished it. They fell in love with one another, and meanwhile I went altogether to the bad, and abandoned my wife of my own accord. And besides, there was Másha. I myself advised them to marry. They did not want to, but I became more and more impossible, and it ended in ...

PETUSHKÓV. The usual thing?

FÉDYA. No. I am sure; I know for certain that they remained pure. He is a religious man, and considers marriage without the Church's blessing a sin. So they began asking me to agree to a divorce. I should have had to take the blame on myself. It would have been necessary to tell all sorts of lies ... and I couldn't! Believe me, it would have been easier for me to take my life than to tell such lies--and I wished to do so. But then a kind friend came and said, "Why do it?" and arranged it all for me. I wrote a farewell letter, and next day my clothes, pocket-book and letters were found on the river bank. I can't swim.

PETUSHKÓV. Yes, but how about the body? They did not find that!

FÉDYA. They did! Fancy! A week later somebody's body was found. My wife was called to identify the decomposing body. She just glanced at it. "Is it he?" "It is." And so it was left. I was buried, and they married and are living in this town, happily. And I--here I am, living and drinking! Yesterday I passed their house. The windows were lit up, and someone's shadow crossed the blind. Sometimes it's horrid, and sometimes not. It's horrid when I've no money ... [Drinks].

ARTÉMYEV [approaches] Excuse me, but I heard your story. It's a very good story, and more than that--a very useful one! You say it's horrid when one has no money? There's nothing more horrid. But you, in your position, should always have money. Aren't you a corpse? Well then ...

FÉDYA. Excuse me! I did not speak to you and don't want your advice.

ARTÉMYEV. But I want to give it! You are a corpse; but suppose you come to life again? Then they, your wife and that gentleman, who are so happy--they would be bigamists, and at best would be sent to the less distant parts of Siberia. So why should you lack money?

FÉDYA. I beg you to leave me alone.

ARTÉMYEV. Simply write a letter. I'll write it for you if you like; only give me their address, and you'll be grateful to me.

FÉDYA. Be off, I tell you! I have told you nothing!

ARTÉMYEV. Yes, you have! Here's my witness. The waiter heard you say you were a corpse.

WAITER. I know nothing about it.

FÉDYA. You scoundrel!

ARTÉMYEV. Am I a scoundrel? Eh, police! I'll give him in charge!

Fédya rises to go, but Artémyev holds him. Enter policeman.

Curtain.

SCENE 2

The ivy-covered verandah of a bungalow in the country. Anna Dmítrievna Karénina. Lisa (pregnant), nurse, and boy.

LISA. Now he's on his way from the station.

BOY. Who is?

LISA. Papa.

BOY. Papa's coming from the station?

LISA. C'est étonnant comme il l'aime, tout-à-fait comme son père.[23]

[23] It is surprising how he loves him--just as if he were his father.

ANNA DMÍTRIEVNA. Tant mieux! Se souvient-il de son père véritable?[24]

[24] So much the better! Does he remember his real father?

LISA [sighs] I never speak to him about it. I say to myself, "Why confuse him?" Sometimes I think I ought to tell him. What is your opinion, *Maman*?

ANNA DMÍTRIEVNA. I think it is a matter of feeling, Lisa, and if you obey your feelings your heart will tell you what to say and when to say it. What a wonderful conciliator death is! I confess there was a time when Fédya--whom I had known from a child--was repulsive to me; but now I only remember him as that nice lad, Victor's friend, and as the passionate man who sacrificed himself--illegally and irreligiously, but still sacrificed himself--for those he loved. On aura beau dire, l'action est belle.[25]... I hope Victor will not forget to bring the wool: I've hardly any left. [Knits].

[25] Say what one likes--it is a fine action.

LISA. I hear him coming.

The sound of wheels and bells is heard. Lisa rises, and goes to the edge of the veranda.

LISA. There's someone with him, a lady in a bonnet--It's Mother! I have not seen her for an age. [Goes to the door].

Enter Karénin and Anna Pávlovna.

ANNA PÁVLOVNA [kisses Lisa and Anna Dmítrievna] Victor met me, and has brought me here.

ANNA DMÍTRIEVNA. He has done well.

ANNA PÁVLOVNA. Yes, certainly. I thought to myself, "When shall I see her again?" and kept putting it off. But now I've come, and if you don't turn me out I will stay till the last train.

KARÉNIN [kisses his wife, mother, and the boy] D'you know what a piece of luck! Congratulate me--I have two days' holiday. They'll be able to get on without me to-morrow.

LISA. Splendid! Two days! It's long since we had that! We'll drive to the Hermitage, shall we?

ANNA PÁVLOVNA. What a likeness! Isn't he a strapping fellow? If only he has not inherited everything--his father's heart ...

ANNA DMÍTRIEVNA. But not his weakness.

LISA. No, everything! Victor agrees with me that if only he had been rightly guided in childhood ...

ANNA PÁVLOVNA. Well, I don't know about that; but I simply can't think of him without tears.

LISA. No more can we. How much higher he stands now in our recollection!

ANNA PÁVLOVNA. Yes, I am sure of it.

LISA. How it all seemed insoluble at one time--and then everything suddenly came right.

ANNA DMÍTRIEVNA. Well, Victor, did you get the wool?

KARÉNIN. Yes, I did. [Brings a bag, and takes out parcels]. Here is the wool, and this is the eau-de-Cologne; and here are letters--one "On Government Service" for you, Lisa [hands her a letter]. Well Anna Pávlovna, if you want to wash your hands I will show you your room. I must make myself tidy too; it is almost dinner time. Lisa, Anna Pávlovna's room is the corner one downstairs, isn't it?

Lisa is pale; holds the letter in trembling hands, and reads it.

KARÉNIN. What's the matter? Lisa, what is it?

LISA. He is alive!... Oh God! When will he release me! Victor, what does this mean? [Sobs].

KARÉNIN [Takes letter and reads] This is dreadful!

ANNA DMÍTRIEVNA. What is it? Why don't you tell me?

KARÉNIN. It is dreadful! He's alive, she's a bigamist, and I a criminal! It's a notice from the Examining Magistrate--a summons for Lisa to appear before him.

ANNA DMÍTRIEVNA. What a dreadful man! Why has he done this?

KARÉNIN. All lies, lies!

LISA. Oh, how I hate him! I don't know what I am saying ... [Exit in tears. Karénin follows her].

ANNA PÁVLOVNA. How is it he's alive?

ANNA DMÍTRIEVNA. All I know is, that as soon as Victor came in contact with this world of mud--they were sure to draw him in too! And so they have. It's all fraud--all lies!

Curtain.

ACT VI

SCENE 1

The room of an Examining Magistrate, who sits at a table talking to Mélnikov. At a side table a clerk is sorting papers.

EXAMINING MAGISTRATE. But I never said anything of the kind to her. She invented it, and now reproaches me.

MÉLNIKOV. She does not reproach you, but is grieved.

EXAMINING MAGISTRATE. All right, I'll come to dinner. But now I have a very interesting case on. [To Clerk] Ask her in.

CLERK. Shall I ask them both?

EXAMINING MAGISTRATE [finishes his cigarette and hides it] No, only Mrs. Karénina, or rather--by her first husband--Protásova.

MÉLNIKOV [going out] Ah, Karénina!

EXAMINING MAGISTRATE. Yes, it's a nasty affair. It's true I am only beginning to look into it, but it's a bad business. Well, good-bye!
[Exit Mélnikov].

Enter Lisa, in black and veiled.

EXAMINING MAGISTRATE. Take a seat, please. [Points to a chair] Believe me, I much regret to have to question you, but we are under the necessity ... Please be calm, and remember that you need not answer my questions. Only, in my opinion, for your own sake--and in fact for everybody's sake--the truth is best. It is always best, even practically.

LISA. I have nothing to conceal.

EXAMINING MAGISTRATE. Well then [looks at paper]--your name, position, religion--all that I have put down. Is it correct?

LISA. Yes.

EXAMINING MAGISTRATE. You are accused of contracting a marriage with another man, knowing your husband to be alive.

LISA. I did not know it.

EXAMINING MAGISTRATE. And also of having persuaded your husband, and bribed him with money, to commit a fraud--a pretended suicide--in order to free yourself of him.

LISA. That is all untrue.

EXAMINING MAGISTRATE. Well then, allow me to put a few questions. Did you send him 1,200 roubles in July of last year?

LISA. It was his own money, the proceeds of the sale of some things of his. At the time I parted from him, and when I was expecting a divorce,

I sent him the money.

EXAMINING MAGISTRATE. Just so! Very well. That money was sent to him on
the 17th of July, two days before his disappearance?

LISA. I think it was on the 17th, but I don't remember.

EXAMINING MAGISTRATE. And why was the application to the Consistorium
for a divorce withdrawn, just at that time--and the lawyer told not to
proceed with the case?

LISA. I don't know.

EXAMINING MAGISTRATE. Well, and when the police asked you to identify
the body, how was it you recognised it as your husband's?

LISA. I was so excited that I did not look at the body, and I felt so
sure it was he, that when they asked me I answered, "I think it is he."

EXAMINING MAGISTRATE. Yes, you did not see well, in consequence of a
very natural excitement. And now may I ask why you have sent a monthly
remittance to Sarátov, the very town where your first husband was
living?

LISA. My husband sent that money, and I cannot say what it was for, as
that is not my secret. But it was not sent to Theodore Vasílyevich, for
we were firmly convinced of his death. That I can say for certain.[26]

[26] Had Tolstoy lived to give a final revision to this play, he would
probably have made it clearer that Karénin sent a monthly payment to
the clockmaker Evgényev, in response to the request contained in the

last letter Fédya addressed to Lisa and himself; and that this money
found its way to Fédya.

EXAMINING MAGISTRATE. Very well. Only allow me to remark, madam,
that
the fact of our being servants of the law does not prevent our being
men; and believe me I quite understand your position and sympathise with
you! You were tied to a man who squandered your property, was
unfaithful--in short, brought misfortune....

LISA. I loved him.

EXAMINING MAGISTRATE. Yes; but still the desire to free yourself was
natural, and you chose this simpler way, without realising that it would
lead you into what is considered a crime--bigamy! I quite understand it.
The judges will understand too; and therefore I advise you to confess
everything.

LISA. I have nothing to confess. I have never lied. [Cries] Do you want
me any longer?

EXAMINING MAGISTRATE. I must ask you to remain here. I will not trouble
you with any more questions. Only kindly read this over and sign it. It
is your deposition. See whether your answers have been correctly taken
down. Please take that seat. [Points to an armchair by the window. To
Clerk] Ask Mr. Karénin to come in.

     Enter Karénin, stern and solemn.

EXAMINING MAGISTRATE. Please take a seat.

KARÉNIN. Thank you! [Remains standing] What do you want of me?

EXAMINING MAGISTRATE. I have to take your deposition.

KARÉNIN. In what capacity?

EXAMINING MAGISTRATE [smiling] I, in the capacity of Examining Magistrate, am obliged to question you in the capacity of an accused person.

KARÉNIN. Indeed! Accused of what?

EXAMINING MAGISTRATE. Of marrying a woman whose husband was alive. However, allow me to question you properly. Kindly sit down.

KARÉNIN. Thank you.

EXAMINING MAGISTRATE. Your name?

KARÉNIN. Victor Karénin.

EXAMINING MAGISTRATE. Your calling?

KARÉNIN. Chamberlain and Member of Council.

EXAMINING MAGISTRATE. Age?

KARÉNIN. Thirty-eight.

EXAMINING MAGISTRATE. Religion?

KARÉNIN. Orthodox; and I have never before been tried or questioned! Well?

EXAMINING MAGISTRATE. Did you know that Theodore Vasílyevich Pro-

tásov
was alive when you married his wife?

KARÉNIN. I did not know it. We were both convinced that he was drowned.

EXAMINING MAGISTRATE. After Protásov's alleged death, to whom in Sarátov
did you send a monthly remittance?

KARÉNIN. I do not wish to reply to that question.

EXAMINING MAGISTRATE. Very well. Why did you send money--1,200
roubles--to Mr. Protásov just before his pretended death on 17th July?

KARÉNIN. That money was given to me by my wife ...

EXAMINING MAGISTRATE. By Mrs. Protásova?

KARÉNIN. ... by my wife, to send to her husband. She considered that
money to be his, and having severed all connection with him, considered
it unfair to keep it.

EXAMINING MAGISTRATE. One more question--why did you withdraw the
application for divorce?

KARÉNIN. Because Theodore Vasílyevich undertook to apply for a divorce,
and wrote me about it.

EXAMINING MAGISTRATE. Have you got his letter?

KARÉNIN. It has been lost.[27]

[27] Karénin does not produce Fédya's letter because it would have

proved connivance in the divorce proceedings.

EXAMINING MAGISTRATE. It is strange that everything which might convince
the Court of the truth of your evidence should either be lost or
non-existent.

KARÉNIN. Do you want anything more?

EXAMINING MAGISTRATE. I want nothing, except to do my duty; but you'll
have to exonerate yourselves, and I have just advised Mrs. Protásova,
and I advise you also, not to try to hide what everyone can see, but to
say what really happened. Especially as Mr. Protásov is in such a
condition that he has already told everything just as it happened, and
will probably do the same in Court, I should advise ...

KARÉNIN. I request you to keep within the limits of your duty, and not
to give me your advice! May we go? [Approaches Lisa, who rises and takes
his arm].

EXAMINING MAGISTRATE. I am very sorry to be obliged to detain you ...
[Karénin looks round in astonishment] Oh, I don't mean that I arrest
you. Though that would make it easier to get at the truth, I shall not
resort to such a measure. I only want to take Protásov's deposition in
your presence, and to confront him with you--which will make it easier
for you to detect any falsehood in what he says. Please take a seat.
Call in Mr. Protásov!

Enter Fédya, dirty and shabby.

FÉDYA [addresses Lisa and Karénin] Lisa! Elisabeth Andréyevna! Victor! I
am not guilty! I wished to act for the best. But if I am guilty ...
forgive me, forgive me! [Bows low to them].

EXAMINING MAGISTRATE. Please to answer my questions.

FÉDYA. Ask, then.

EXAMINING MAGISTRATE. Your name?

FÉDYA. Why, you know it!

EXAMINING MAGISTRATE. Please answer.

FÉDYA. Well then, Theodore Protásov.

EXAMINING MAGISTRATE. Your calling, age and religion?

FÉDYA [after a pause] Aren't you ashamed to ask such nonsense? Ask what you want to know, and not such rubbish!

EXAMINING MAGISTRATE. I beg you to be more careful in your expressions, and to answer my questions!

FÉDYA. Well, if you're not ashamed of it, here you are: Calling, graduate; age, forty; religion, Orthodox. What next!

EXAMINING MAGISTRATE. Did Mr. Karénin and your wife know that you were
alive when you left your clothes on the river bank and disappeared?

FÉDYA. Certainly not! I wished really to commit suicide, but afterwards--but there's no need to go into that. The thing is, that they knew nothing about it.

EXAMINING MAGISTRATE. How is it that you gave a different account to the police officer?

FÉDYA. What police officer? Oh, when he came to see me at the dosshouse? I was drunk, and was romancing. I don't remember what I said. All that was rubbish. Now I am not drunk, and am telling the whole truth! They knew nothing. They believed that I was no longer alive, and I was glad of it. And everything would have gone on as it was, but for that rascal, Artémyev! If anyone is guilty, it is I alone.

EXAMINING MAGISTRATE. I understand your wish to be magnanimous, but the
law demands the truth. Why was money sent to you?

Fédya is silent.

You received through Semyónov the money sent to you in Sarátov?

Fédya is silent.

Why don't you answer? It will be put down in the depositions that the accused did not answer these questions, and this may harm you and them very much. Well then, how was it?

FÉDYA [after a pause] Oh, Mr. Magistrate, how is it you are not ashamed! Why do you pry into other people's lives? You are glad to have power, and to show it, you torment not physically but morally--torment people a thousand times better than yourself!

EXAMINING MAGISTRATE. I beg ...

FÉDYA. You've nothing to beg! I shall say what I think, and you [to Clerk] write it down! At least for once there will be sensible human words in a police report! [Raises his voice] There are three people: I,

he, and she. Our relations to one another are complex--a spiritual
struggle such as you know nothing of, a struggle between good and evil
goes on. That struggle ends in a manner which sets them free. They were
all at peace. They were happy, and remembered me with affection. I,
fallen as I was, was glad that I had acted as I ought, and that I, a
good-for-nothing, had gone out of their lives, so as not to stand in the
way of people who were good and who had life before them. And so we were
all living, when suddenly a blackmailing scoundrel appears who wants me
to take part in his rascality, and I send him about his business. Then
he comes to you, to the champion of Justice! The guardian of Morality!
And you, who receive each month a few pounds for doing your dirty work,
put on your uniform, and calmly bully these people--bully people whose
little finger is worth more than your whole body and soul! People who
would not admit you to their anteroom! But you have got so far, and are
pleased ...

EXAMINING MAGISTRATE. I shall have you turned out!

FÉDYA. I'm not afraid of anyone, because I'm a corpse and you can't do
me any harm. No position could be worse than mine! So turn me out!

KARÉNIN. May we go?

EXAMINING MAGISTRATE. Immediately, but first sign your deposition.

FÉDYA. You'd be quite comic, if you weren't so vile!

EXAMINING MAGISTRATE. Take him away! I arrest you.

FÉDYA [to Lisa and Karénin] Forgive me!

KARÉNIN [approaches and holds out his hand] It had to happen!

Lisa passes by. Fédya bows low to her.

Curtain.

SCENE 2

A corridor of the Law Courts. In the background a door with glass panels, beside which stands an usher. Further to the right another door through which the accused are led.

Iván Petróvich Alexándrov comes to the first door and wishes to enter.

USHER. Where are you going? You mustn't! Shoving in like that!

IVÁN PETRÓVICH. Why mustn't I? The law says the proceedings are public. [Applause is heard from inside the Court].

USHER. Anyhow, you mustn't, and that's all about it.

IVÁN PETRÓVICH. Ignorant fellow! You don't know whom you are speaking to!

A Young Lawyer in a dress-suit enters from the Court.

YOUNG LAWYER. Are you concerned in this case?

IVÁN PETRÓVICH. No, I am the public, and this ignoramus--this Cerberus--won't let me in!

YOUNG LAWYER. But this door is not for the public.

IVÁN PETRÓVICH. I know, but I am a man who should be admitted.

YOUNG LAWYER. Wait a bit--they'll adjourn in a minute. [Is just going, when he meets Prince Abrézkov].

PRINCE ABRÉZKOV. May I ask how the case stands?

YOUNG LAWYER. The Counsel are speaking--Petrúshin is addressing the Court.

　　　Applause from within.

PRINCE ABRÉZKOV. And how do the defendants bear their position?

YOUNG LAWYER. With great dignity, especially Karénin and Elisabeth Andréyevna. It is as if not they were being indicted, but they were indicting society! That's what is felt, and on that Petrúshin is working.

PRINCE ABRÉZKOV. Well, and Protásov?

YOUNG LAWYER. He is terribly excited. He trembles all over; but that is natural, considering the life he leads. He is particularly irritable, and interrupted the Public Prosecutor and Counsel several times ...

PRINCE ABRÉZKOV. What do you think the result will be?

YOUNG LAWYER. It is hard to say. In any case they won't be found guilty of premeditation; but still ... [A gentleman comes out, and Prince Abrézkov moves towards the door] You wish to go in?

PRINCE ABRÉZKOV. I should like to.

YOUNG LAWYER. You are Prince Abrézkov?

PRINCE ABRÉZKOV. I am.

YOUNG LAWYER [to Usher] Let this gentleman pass. There is an empty chair just to the left.

> Usher lets Prince Abrézkov pass. As the door opens, Counsel is seen speaking.

IVÁN PETRÓVICH. Aristocrats! I am an aristocrat of the soul, and that is higher!

YOUNG LAWYER. Well, excuse me ... [Exit].

> Petushkóv enters hurriedly, and approaches Iván Petróvich.

PETUSHKÓV. Ah, how are you, Iván Petróvich? How are things going?

IVÁN PETRÓVICH. Counsel are still speaking, but this fellow won't let me in.

USHER. Don't make a noise here! This is not a public-house!

> Applause. The doors open. Lawyers, and the public--men and women--come out.

A LADY. Splendid! He really moved me to tears.

OFFICER. It's better than any novel. Only I don't understand how she could love him so. Dreadful object!

The other door opens. The accused come out: first Lisa, then Karénin. They pass along the corridor. Fédya follows alone.

LADY. Hush--here he is! Look how excited he seems!

Lady and Officer pass on.

FÉDYA [approaches Iván Petróvich] Have you brought it?

IVÁN PETRÓVICH. Here it is. [Hands Fédya something].

FÉDYA [Hides it in his pocket, and wishes to pass out, but sees Petushkóv] Stupid! Vile! Dreary, dreary! Senseless. [Wishes to pass].

Enter Counsel Petrúshin; stout, red, and animated. He approaches Fédya.

PETRÚSHIN. Well, friend! Our affairs are going well--only don't you go and spoil things for me in your last speech!

FÉDYA. I won't speak. What is the use? I shan't do it.

PETRÚSHIN. Yes, you must speak. But don't be excited. The whole matter is now in a nutshell! Only tell them what you told me--that if you are being tried, it is only for *not* having committed suicide: that is, for not doing what is considered a crime both by civil and ecclesiastical law.

FÉDYA. I shan't say anything!

PETRÚSHIN. Why not?

FÉDYA. I don't want to, and shan't. Tell me only, at the worst, what will it be?

PETRÚSHIN. I have already told you--at worst, exile to Siberia.

FÉDYA. Who will be exiled?

PETRÚSHIN. You and your wife.

FÉDYA. And at best?

PETRÚSHIN. Church penance, and of course annulment of the second marriage.

FÉDYA. Then they will again tie me to her--or rather, her to me?

PETRÚSHIN. Yes, that must be so. But don't excite yourself, and please say what I told you, and above all, don't say anything superfluous. However [noticing that a circle of listeners has formed round them] I am tired, and will go and sit down; and you'd better take a rest. The chief thing is, not to lose courage!

FÉDYA. No other sentence is possible?

PETRÚSHIN [going] No other.

Enter Attendant.

ATTENDANT. Pass on! Pass on! No loitering in the corridor!

FÉDYA. Directly! [Takes out revolver and shoots himself in the heart. Falls. All rush on him] All right, I think it is done.... Lisa!...

The audience, judges, accused, and witnesses rush out from all the doors.

In front of all is Lisa. Behind her Másha, Karénin, Iván Petróvich and Prince Abrézkov.

LISA. Fédya, what have you done! Why?

FÉDYA. Forgive me that I could not ... free you any other way.... It's not for you ... it's best for me. I have long ... been ready ...

LISA. You will live!

A Doctor bends over Fédya and listens.

FÉDYA. I need no doctor to tell me ... Good-bye, Victor ... Ah, Másha!... it's too late this time ... [Weeps] How good ... how good! [Dies].

Curtain.

END OF "THE LIVE CORPSE."

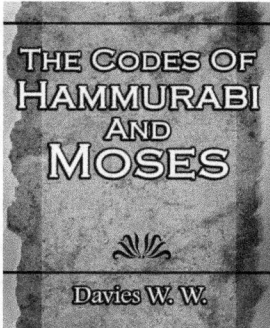

The Codes Of Hammurabi And Moses
W. W. Davies

QTY

The discovery of the Hammurabi Code is one of the greatest achievements of archaeology, and is of paramount interest, not only to the student of the Bible, but also to all those interested in ancient history...

Religion   **ISBN:** *1-59462-338-4*   **Pages:132**

MSRP $12.95

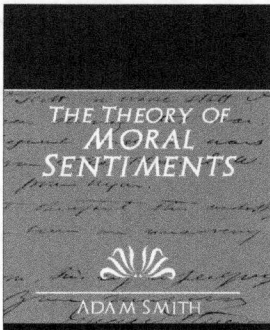

The Theory of Moral Sentiments
Adam Smith

QTY

This work from 1749. contains original theories of conscience amd moral judgment and it is the foundation for systemof morals.

Philosophy **ISBN:** *1-59462-777-0*   **Pages:536**

MSRP $19.95

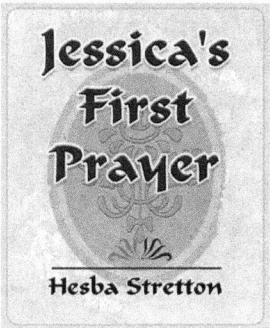

Jessica's First Prayer
Hesba Stretton

QTY

In a screened and secluded corner of one of the many railway-bridges which span the streets of London there could be seen a few years ago, from five o'clock every morning until half past eight, a tidily set-out coffee-stall, consisting of a trestle and board, upon which stood two large tin cans, with a small fire of charcoal burning under each so as to keep the coffee boiling during the early hours of the morning when the work-people were thronging into the city on their way to their daily toil...

Pages:84

Childrens   **ISBN:** *1-59462-373-2*   *MSRP $9.95*

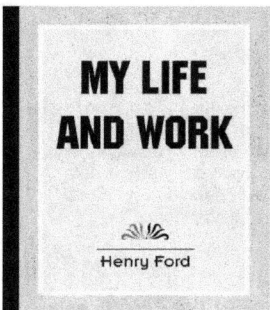

My Life and Work
Henry Ford

QTY

Henry Ford revolutionized the world with his implementation of mass production for the Model T automobile. Gain valuable business insight into his life and work with his own auto-biography... "We have only started on our development of our country we have not as yet, with all our talk of wonderful progress, done more than scratch the surface. The progress has been wonderful enough but..."

Pages:300

Biographies/ **ISBN:** *1-59462-198-5*   *MSRP $21.95*

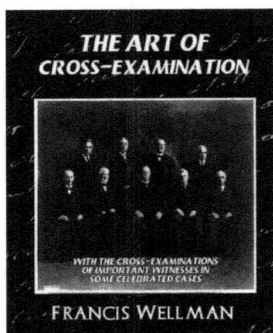

The Art of Cross-Examination
Francis Wellman

I presume it is the experience of every author, after his first book is published upon an important subject, to be almost overwhelmed with a wealth of ideas and illustrations which could readily have been included in his book, and which to his own mind, at east, seem to make a second edition inevitable. Such certainly was the case with me; and when the first edition had reached its sixth impression in five months, I rejoiced to learn that it seemed to my publishers that the book had met with a sufficiently favorable reception to justify a second and considerably enlarged edition. ..

Pages:412

Reference   ISBN: *1-59462-647-2*   *MSRP $19.95*

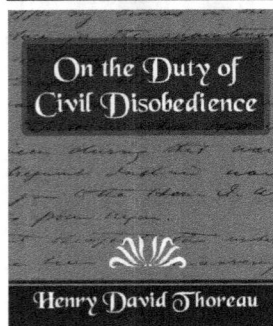

On the Duty of Civil Disobedience
Henry David Thoreau

Thoreau wrote his famous essay, On the Duty of Civil Disobedience, as a protest against an unjust but popular war and the immoral but popular institution of slave-owning. He did more than write—he declined to pay his taxes, and was hauled off to gaol in consequence. Who can say how much this refusal of his hastened the end of the war and of slavery ?

Law   ISBN: *1-59462-747-9*

Pages:48

MSRP $7.45

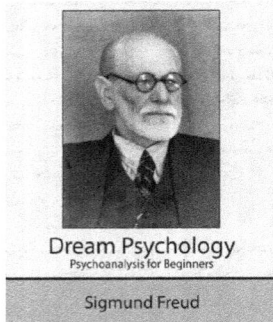

Dream Psychology Psychoanalysis for Beginners
Sigmund Freud

Sigmund Freud, born Sigismund Schlomo Freud (May 6, 1856 - September 23, 1939), was a Jewish-Austrian neurologist and psychiatrist who co-founded the psychoanalytic school of psychology. Freud is best known for his theories of the unconscious mind, especially involving the mechanism of repression; his redefinition of sexual desire as mobile and directed towards a wide variety of objects; and his therapeutic techniques, especially his understanding of transference in the therapeutic relationship and the presumed value of dreams as sources of insight into unconscious desires.

Pages:196

Psychology   ISBN: *1-59462-905-6*   *MSRP $15.45*

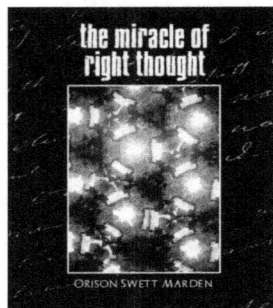

The Miracle of Right Thought
Orison Swett Marden

Believe with all of your heart that you will do what you were made to do. When the mind has once formed the habit of holding cheerful, happy, prosperous pictures, it will not be easy to form the opposite habit. It does not matter how improbable or how far away this realization may see, or how dark the prospects may be, if we visualize them as best we can, as vividly as possible, hold tenaciously to them and vigorously struggle to attain them, they will gradually become actualized, realized in the life. But a desire, a longing without endeavor, a yearning abandoned or held ind fferently will vanish without realization.

Pages:360

Self Help   ISBN: *1-59462-644-8*   *MSRP $25.45*

The Rosicrucian Cosmo-Conception Mystic Christianity *by Max Heindel*   ISBN: *1-59462-188-8*   **$38.95**
The Rosicrucian Cosmo-conception is not dogmatic, neither does it appeal to any other authority than the reason of the student. It is: not controversial, but is: sent forth in the, hope that it may help to clear...   New Age/Religion Pages 646

Abandonment To Divine Providence *by Jean-Pierre de Caussade*   ISBN: *1-59462-228-0*   **$25.95**
"The Rev. Jean Pierre de Caussade was one of the most remarkable spiritual writers of the Society of Jesus in France in the 18th Century. His death took place at Toulouse in 1751. His works have gone through many editions and have been republished...   Inspirational/Religion Pages 400

Mental Chemistry *by Charles Haanel*   ISBN: *1-59462-192-6*   **$23.95**
Mental Chemistry allows the change of material conditions by combining and appropriately utilizing the power of the mind. Much like applied chemistry creates something new and unique out of careful combinations of chemicals the mastery of mental chemistry...   New Age/Business Pages 354

The Letters of Robert Browning and Elizabeth Barret Barrett 1845-1846 vol II   ISBN: *1-59462-193-4*   **$35.95**
by Robert Browning and Elizabeth Barrett   Biographies Pages 596

Gleanings In Genesis (volume I) *by Arthur W. Pink*   ISBN: *1-59462-130-6*   **$27.45**
Appropriately has Genesis been termed "the seed plot of the Bible" for in it we have, in germ form, almost all of the great doctrines which are afterwards fully developed in the books of Scripture which follow...   Religion/Inspirational Pages 420

The Master Key *by L. W. de Laurence*   ISBN: *1-59462-001-6*   **$30.95**
In no branch of human knowledge has there been a more lively increase of the spirit of research during the past few years than in the study of Psychology, Concentration and Mental Discipline. The requests for authentic lessons in Thought Control, Mental Discipline and...   New Age/Occult Pages 422

The Lesser Key Of Solomon Goetia *by L. W. de Laurence*   ISBN: *1-59462-092-X*   **$9.95**
This translation of the first book of the "Lernegton" which is now for the first time made accessible to students of Talismanic Magic was done, after careful collation and edition, from numerous Ancient Manuscripts in Hebrew, Latin, and French...   New Age/Occult Pages 92

Rubaiyat Of Omar Khayyam *by Edward Fitzgerald*   ISBN: *1-59462-332-5*   **$13.95**
Edward Fitzgerald, whom the world has already learned, in spite of his own efforts to remain within the shadow of anonymity, to look upon as one of the rarest poets of the century, was born at Bredfield, in Suffolk, on the 31st of March, 1809. He was the third son of John Purcell...   Music Pages 172

Ancient Law *by Henry Maine*   ISBN: *1-59462-128-4*   **$29.95**
The chief object of the following pages is to indicate some of the earliest ideas of mankind. as they are reflected in Ancient Law, and to point out the relation of those ideas to modern thought.   Religiom/History Pages 452

Far-Away Stories *by William J. Locke*   ISBN: *1-59462-129-2*   **$19.45**
"Good wine needs no bush, but a collection of mixed vintages does. And this book is just such a collection. Some of the stories I do not want to remain buried for ever in the museum files of dead magazine-numbers an author's not unpardonable vanity..."   Fiction Pages 272

Life of David Crockett *by David Crockett*   ISBN: *1-59462-250-7*   **$27.45**
"Colonel David Crockett was one of the most remarkable men of the times in which he lived. Born in humble life, but gifted with a strong will, an indomitable courage, and unremitting perseverance...   Biographies/New Age Pages 424

Lip-Reading *by Edward Nitchie*   ISBN: *1-59462-206-X*   **$25.95**
Edward B. Nitchie, founder of the New York School for the Hard of Hearing, now the Nitchie School of Lip-Reading, Inc, wrote "LIP-READING Principles and Practice". The development and perfecting of this meritorious work on lip-reading was an undertaking...   How-to Pages 400

A Handbook of Suggestive Therapeutics, Applied Hypnotism, Psychic Science   ISBN: *1-59462-214-0*   **$24.95**
by Henry Munro   Health/New Age/Health/Self-help Pages 376

A Doll's House: and Two Other Plays *by Henrik Ibsen*   ISBN: *1-59462-112-8*   **$19.95**
Henrik Ibsen created this classic when in revolutionary 1848 Rome. Introducing some striking concepts in playwriting for the realist genre, this play has been studied the world over.   Fiction/Classics/Plays 308

The Light of Asia *by sir Edwin Arnold*   ISBN: *1-59462-204-3*   **$13.95**
In this poetic masterpiece, Edwin Arnold describes the life and teachings of Buddha. The man who was to become known as Buddha to the world was born as Prince Gautama of India but he rejected the worldly riches and abandoned the reigns of power when...   Religion/History/Biographies Pages 170

The Complete Works of Guy de Maupassant *by Guy de Maupassant*   ISBN: *1-59462-157-8*   **$16.95**
"For days and days, nights and nights, I had dreamed of that first kiss which was to consecrate our engagement, and I knew not on what spot I should put my lips..."   Fiction/Classics Pages 240

The Art of Cross-Examination *by Francis L. Wellman*   ISBN: *1-59462-309-0*   **$26.95**
Written by a renowned trial lawyer, Wellman imparts his experience and uses case studies to explain how to use psychology to extract desired information through questioning.   How-to/Science/Reference Pages 408

Answered or Unanswered? *by Louisa Vaughan*   ISBN: *1-59462-248-5*   **$10.95**
Miracles of Faith in China   Religion Pages 112

The Edinburgh Lectures on Mental Science (1909) *by Thomas*   ISBN: *1-59462-008-3*   **$11.95**
This book contains the substance of a course of lectures recently given by the writer in the Queen Street Hall, Edinburgh. Its purpose is to indicate the Natural Principles governing the relation between Mental Action and Material Conditions ..   New Age/Psychology Pages 148

Ayesha *by H. Rider Haggard*   ISBN: *1-59462-301-5*   **$24.95**
Verily and indeed it is the unexpected that happens! Probably if there was one person upon the earth from whom the Editor of this, and of a certain previous history, did not expect to hear again...   Classics Pages 380

Ayala's Angel *by Anthony Trollope*   ISBN: *1-59462-352-X*   **$29.95**
The two girls were both pretty, but Lucy who was twenty-one who supposed to be simple and comparatively unattractive, whereas Ayala was credited, as her Bombwhat romantic name might show, with poetic charm and a taste for romance. Ayala when her father died was nineteen...   Fiction Pages 484

The American Commonwealth *by James Bryce*   ISBN: *1-59462-286-8*   **$34.45**
An interpretation of American democratic political theory. It examines political mechanics and society from the perspective of Scotsman James Bryce   Politics Pages 572

Stories of the Pilgrims *by Margaret P. Pumphrey*   ISBN: *1-59462-116-0*   **$17.95**
This book explores pilgrims religious oppression in England as well as their escape to Holland and eventual crossing to America on the Mayflower, and their early days in New England...   History Pages 268

QTY

The Fasting Cure *by Sinclair Upton*   ISBN: *1-59462-222-1*   **$13.95**
In the Cosmopolitan Magazine for May, 1910, and in the Contemporary Review (London) for April, 1910, I published an article dealing with my experiences in fasting. I have written a great many magazine articles, but never one which attracted so much attention...   New Age/Self Help/Health Pages 164

Hebrew Astrology *by Sepharial*   ISBN: *1-59462-308-2*   **$13.45**
In these days of advanced thinking it is a matter of common observation that we have left many of the old landmarks behind and that we are now pressing forward to greater heights and to a wider horizon than that which represented the mind-content of our progenitors...   Astrology Pages 144

Thought Vibration or The Law of Attraction in the Thought World   ISBN: *1-59462-127-6*   **$12.95**
by William Walker Atkinson   Psychology/Religion Pages 144

Optimism *by Helen Keller*   ISBN: *1-59462-108-X*   **$15.95**
Helen Keller was blind, deaf, and mute since 19 months old, yet famously learned how to overcome these handicaps, communicate with the world, and spread her lectures promoting optimism. An inspiring read for everyone...   Biographies/Inspirational Pages 84

Sara Crewe *by Frances Burnett*   ISBN: *1-59462-360-0*   **$9.45**
In the first place, Miss Minchin lived in London. Her home was a large, dull, tall one, in a large, dull square, where all the houses were alike, and all the sparrows were alike, and where all the door-knockers made the same heavy sound...   Childrens/Classic Pages 88

The Autobiography of Benjamin Franklin *by Benjamin Franklin*   ISBN: *1-59462-135-7*   **$24.95**
The Autobiography of Benjamin Franklin has probably been more extensively read than any other American historical work, and no other book of its kind has had such ups and downs of fortune. Franklin lived for many years in England, where he was agent...   Biographies/History Pages 332

Name	
Email	
Telephone	
Address	
City, State ZIP	

☐ **Credit Card**   ☐ **Check / Money Order**

Credit Card Number	
Expiration Date	
Signature	

Please Mail to: Book Jungle
PO Box 2226
Champaign, IL 61825
or Fax to: 630-214-0564

ORDERING INFORMATION

web: *www.bookjungle.com*
email: *sales@bookjungle.com*
fax: *630-214-0564*
mail: *Book Jungle PO Box 2226 Champaign, IL 61825*
or PayPal *to sales@bookjungle.com*

Please contact us for bulk discounts

DIRECT-ORDER TERMS

**20% Discount if You Order
Two or More Books**
Free Domestic Shipping!
Accepted: Master Card, Visa,
Discover, American Express

www.ingramcontent.com/pod-product-compliance
Lightning Source LLC
LaVergne TN
LVHW081324060426
835511LV00011B/1848